D0612967

THE TRAUMA
OF TRANSGRESSION

COMMENTARY

Incest conjures the most powerful reactions in the participants, as well as in those who treat these children and adults, and those who research the subject. Drs. Kramer and Akhtar have edited a fascinating, remarkable, and very valuable contribution to the analytic and psychotherapy literature. The breadth and depth of exploration and explanation by informed and original authors is outstanding, and includes the predisposition to incest, the causes and consequences of the trauma of incest, and long range follow-up of incest cases. Discussion of the chapters and the integrative technical and theoretical essays of the editors enrich and bridge the many concepts and ideas that appear throughout the anthology. This book is recommended to all therapists and students who want to expand their knowledge of incest, and access current analytic thought on the sexual abuse of children.

—Harold Blum, M.D.

The Trauma of Transgression is about the analytic psychotherapy of incest. It reflects a contemporary ego psychology developmentally informed by the object relations theory of Margaret Mahler. Rich in clinical wisdom and lucid in analytic theory, this volume offers mental health professionals access to detailed case studies and sophisticated discussions in the psychoanalysis and analytic psychotherapy of incest victims. It should deepen the appreciation of all practitioners to the challenges of analytic therapy with the victims of incest and hold an important place among the recently emerging psychoanalytic contributions to the recognition, understanding, and treatment of incest.

—Howard B. Levine, M.D.

The recent interest in childhood abuse has resulted in voluminous literature on incest by mental health professionals. This book, however, is unique. It brings together the clinical, theoretical, and technical findings of seven psychoanalysts and opens a door to the intrapsychic worlds of incest victims as well as their family members. The more we learn about the details and the nuances of the psychopathology of incest, the more we make inroads into its prevention and treatment.

—Vamık D. Volkan, M.D.

THE TRAUMA OF TRANSGRESSION
Psychotherapy of Incest Victims

edited by

SELMA KRAMER, M.D., and
SALMAN AKHTAR, M.D.

JASON ARONSON INC.
Northvale, New Jersey
London

Copyright © 1991 by Jason Aronson Inc.

10 9 8 7 6 5 4 3 2 1

All rights reserved. Printed in the United States of America. No part of this book may be used or reproduced in any manner whatsoever without written permission from Jason Aronson Inc. except in the case of brief quotations in reviews for inclusion in a magazine, newspaper, or broadcast.

Production and interior design: *Gloria Jordan*
Editorial Director: *Muriel Jorgensen*

This book was set in 12/14 Bembo
by Alpha Graphics in Pittsfield, New Hampshire
and printed and bound by Haddon Craftsmen in Scranton, Pennsylvania

Library of Congress Cataloging-in-Publication Data

The Trauma of transgression : psychotherapy of incest victims / edited
   by Selma Kramer & Salman Akhtar.
         p.   cm.
      Papers from the 21st Annual Margaret S. Mahler Symposium on Child
   Development, held in Philadelphia, May 19, 1990.
      Includes bibliographical references.
      Includes index.
      ISBN 0-87668-554-8
      1. Incest victims—Mental health—Congresses.   2. Adult child
   sexual abuse victims—Mental health—Congresses.   3. Incest-
   Psychological aspects—Congresses.   4. Incest victims—Mental
   health—Case studies—Congresses.   5. Psychotherapy—Congresses.
   I. Kramer, Selma.   II. Akhtar, Salman, 1946 July 31–   III. Margaret
   S. Mahler Symposium on Child Development (21st : 1990 :
   Philadelphia, Pa.)
      [DNLM: 1. Incest—psychology.   2. Psychotherapy—methods.   WM 610
   T777]
   RC560.I53T72   1991
   616.85′83—dc20
   DNLM/DLC
   for Library of Congress   91-4565

Manufactured in the United States of America. Jason Aronson Inc. offers books and cassettes. For information and catalog write to Jason Aronson Inc., 230 Livingston Street, Northvale, New Jersey 07647.

To the memory
of Margaret S. Mahler
teacher, friend, source of inspiration

Contents

Acknowledgment

The chapters in this book were originally papers presented at the Twenty-first Annual Margaret S. Mahler Symposium on Child Development held on May 19, 1990, in Philadelphia. First and foremost, therefore, we wish to express our gratitude to the Margaret S. Mahler Psychiatric Research Foundation. We are also grateful to Troy L. Thompson II, M.D., chairman, Department of Psychiatry and Human Behavior, Jefferson Medical College, as well as to the Philadelphia Psychoanalytic Institute and Society for their shared sponsorship of this symposium. Many colleagues from the Institute and Society helped during the symposium and we remain grateful to them. Finally, we wish to acknowledge our sincere appreciation of Ms. Gloria Schwartz for her efficient organizational assistance during the symposium and outstanding skills in the preparation of this book's manuscript.

Contributors

Salman Akhtar, M.D.
Professor of Psychiatry, Jefferson Medical College; Faculty, Philadelphia Psychoanalytic Institue, Philadelphia, Pennsylvania.

Maurice Apprey, Ph.D.
Associate Professor of Psychiatry, Assistant Dean, Student Affairs, University of Virginia School of Medicine, Charlottesville, Virginia.

M. Hossein Etezady, M.D.
Clinical Director of Psychiatric Services, Paoli Memorial Hospital, Paoli, Pennsylvania; President, Regional Council of Child and Adolescent Psychiatry; Faculty, Philadelphia Psychoanalytic Institute, Philadelphia, Pennsylvania.

Ruth M. S. Fischer, M.D.
President, Philadelphia Psychoanalytic Society; Training and Supervising Analyst, Philadelphia Psychoanalytic Institute; Faculty,

University of Pennsylvania School of Medicine, Philadelphia, Pennsylvania.

Selma Kramer, M.D.

Professor of Psychiatry, Jefferson Medical College; Training and Supervising Analyst, Philadelphia Psychoanalytic Institute, Philadelphia, Pennsylvania.

Marvin Margolis, M.D., Ph.D.

Clinical Associate Professor of Psychiatry, College of Medicine, Wayne State University; Training and Supervising Analyst, Michigan Psychoanalytic Institute, Southfield, Michigan.

Brandt F. Steele, M.D.

Professor of Psychiatry, Emeritus, University of Colorado Health Sciences Center; Consultant, Kempe National Center for Prevention of Child Abuse and Neglect; Training Analyst, Denver Institute for Psychoanalysis, Denver, Colorado.

PSYCHOPATHOLOGICAL EFFECTS OF INCEST

Selma Kramer, M.D.

What is the significance of the recent increase in psychoanalytic publications about incest? Does it reflect an actual increase in the occurrence of incest? Some of my colleagues think it does and attribute it to the sexual revolution. They assert that the breakdown of sexual barriers between adults has led to a parallel rupture of such barriers between parents and children. While plausible, this explanation does not account for all the facts. Certainly the molested patients encountered by Ferenczi (1933) were not the children of the sexual revolution, nor were those reported in the early papers of Margolis (1977, 1984), Shengold (1967, 1974), or Steele (1970, 1981). I propose that incest (as well as the taboo against it) has been around as far back as families have existed. I contend that there are more reports of incest now because we listen to our patients more carefully, interpret with greater precision, and are more alert to nuances of transference and countertransference in such cases. As we are more ready to do this with our patients, we similarly have become more able to recognize the existence of certain configurations that suggest maternal or paternal incest in cases we supervise.

Incest occurs in dysfunctional families. It can be safely said that dysfunctional mothers seldom are able to provide the young infant with the emotional supplies necessary for a gratifying symbiosis. As a result, the foundation for his developing basic trust is weakened, and the stepping-stone from which separation–individuation would ordinarily follow remains wobbly, so to speak. A dysfunctional father, on the other hand, cannot carry out his important role of assuring an environment of safety for the growing child. He is not an object for healthy identification, nor does he help extricate a child from a too-close relationship with the mother. Early sexual abuse from either parent disrupts the normal separation–individuation sequence; it seems to have a particularly disruptive effect on rapprochement subphase issues. Consequently, abused children manifest a great vulnerability to separation problems, depression, and splitting of good and bad self and good and bad object. Incest causes the shared parental and self omnipotence to become distorted, leaving the child to experience unmanageable amounts of excitement, undue anger, and an overall sense of impotence. Symbolic thinking, as well as reality testing, are compromised because parents do one thing while they say they do another. The parents' use of denial and their foisting responsibility for the sexual acts upon the child create confusion in the mind of the child, who is then unable to trust his or her own perceptions. The child, normally self-centered at that age, too easily accepts the onus for the parental sexual molestation and is further burdened by the secrecy imposed by the parent.

Mahler's theories of development in the first three years dovetail with Freud's theories of development (Kramer and Akhtar 1988, Parens 1980, Pine 1986). Her findings add to and interdigitate with Freud's, as seen in her description (Mahler 1971, 1972) of the child in the rapprochement subphase as being vulnerable and burdened because of continuing oral phase pressures and the need to deal with the tasks and ambivalence of the anal phase, together with conflicts introduced by beginnings of the oedipal phase. Traumata during the separation–individuation process inevitably compromise the ability of the child to resolve the oedipal conflict. At the 1973 Paris panel, Mahler (1975), together with Ritvo (1974), Lebovici (1973), and Loewald (1974), agreed that the "shape" of the Oedipus complex and the infantile neurosis does not arise anew but settles on the anlage formed by the psychic structure already in place in the preoedipal child.

Where incest occurs in later childhood or in adolescence, the parents have generally not been "good enough" in the child's earliest developmental stages. Even where this is not so, incest in the latency, prepubertal, or adolescent developmental stages leads to confusion, regression, guilt, and to the feeling of being vulnerable to abuse by parents who fail to fulfill their normal protective functions. In such adolescents, the "second individuation" (Blos 1967) or the normal phase-specific regression that eventually loosens infantile ties to primary love objects and enables movement toward healthy adulthood fails to occur. If this regression takes the adolescent back to an early, unstable intrapsychic situation, it is unlikely that the second individuation will parallel genital maturation. Under such circumstances, the ego–ideal is not realistically transformed during adolescence. The superego retains its primitive parental features and fails to cope with resurgent drives and new realities because of intractable identifications with the faulty parental superegos. Adolescents who have been sexually abused during childhood or adolescence often manifest eating disorders, proclivity to masochistic and self-destructive behavior like cutting themselves, or a multiple personality disorder (Kluft 1990, Putnam 1986). These syndromes represent regression to earlier oral and anal developmental phases, with an upsurge of ambivalence and a regression to the pathological defense of splitting. Anorexia very often goes hand in hand with age-inappropriate immaturity and with severe separation problems (Fischer 1989). Naked, unmodulated aggression against the self is seen in the form of depression, self-mutilation, or self-starvation, or against others in the form of outbursts of rage or destructive behavior.

A developmental achievement often compromised when incest occurs early (with either parent) is the attainment of object constancy, at which time, in normal development, a fusion of good and bad self and good and bad object should have been attained. The lack of this fusion contributes to a prolonged and costly dependency on the primary love objects (usually the mother, even if she is the molester). I can only speculate how frequently, already in adolescence, an abused child becomes the sexual abuser of others. Many abused adolescents (both males and females) run away from home to a life of prostitution.

I have found it significant that following molestation in early development by their mothers, many adolescents and adults of both sexes fear the sexual abuse means that they, the victims of incest, are homosexual. Boys molested by their fathers experience especially deep humiliation, shame, and anger; they feel that to be molested by a male means that they are homosexual, and they are conflicted speculating whether or not their fathers are homosexual. Girls molested by their fathers may become homosexual as a defense against their strong heterosexual stirrings or as an angry response to their fathers' sexual abuse. Other girls, who feel that sexual abuse is the only positive attention they receive from males, may frantically and futilely seek relief from their pain through promiscuous sex.

In the comments that follow, I largely share my own clinical observations in this realm rather than offer a comprehensive review of literature. However, I do wish to state that while Freud's moving away from the "seduction theory" to the discovery of the Oedipus complex is well known, it is often forgotten that he never overlooked the fact that some children had indeed been molested by their parents. He stated (1931) that actual seduction was common, and "when seduction intervenes it invariably disturbs the natural course of the developmental processes, and it often leaves behind extensive and lasting consequences" (p. 232). Freud (1932) added

> . . . I was able to recognize in this phantasy of being seduced by
> the father the expression of the typical oedipus complex in
> women. And now we find the phantasy of seduction once more
> in the pre-oedipus prehistory of girls; but the seducer is regularly
> the mother. Here, however, the phantasy touches the ground of
> reality, for it was really the mother who by her activities over
> the child's bodily hygiene inevitably stimulated, and perhaps
> even roused for the first time, pleasurable sensations in her
> genitals. [p. 120]

I became interested in some rather subtle psychopathological effects of incest when a patient manifested a type of thinking I had encountered only twice before. As I reviewed the cases, two of which I had reported (Kramer 1974, 1980) to demonstrate their backgrounds, their intrapsychic problems, and their analyses, I recognized an important element common to all three. Each patient had experienced "maternal incest," that is, their mothers had masturbated them from infancy, probably as an outgrowth of earlier care for their hygiene. The psychopathologic effect of such maternal overstimulation was a unique form of doubting I called "object coercive doubting" (Kramer 1983). My patients attempted to coerce me in the maternal transference to argue for one of the two sides of their intrapsychic conflict. Such conflicts were usually about knowing. For instance, a patient who had repeatedly been exposed to her parents' genitals once asked me if I were wearing an initial pin on my lapel. Since it was quite obvious that I was, I did not actually answer the question. The patient became increasingly upset and insisted that I tell her that I was indeed wearing the pin. Another patient felt his lips and nose to be getting alternately bigger and smaller (a thinly disguised equivalent of tumescence and detumescence) during a session. While having this feeling himself, he insisted that I tell him that this was indeed happening. In both these instances, the patients were attempting to force me to take one side of the conflict they were experiencing. I feel that this transference phenomenon derived from a lack of differentiation, a failure to intrapsychically separate from the mother–child dual unity. I regard it as distinct from obsessional doubting, which results from a well-internalized, structural conflict.

In addition, all three patients showed much conflict about physical separation from their parents. In the course of their analyses it became obvious that my patients controlled their parents' freedom by their supposed need for help with homework. The parents, to my surprise, were extremely compliant in response to their children's control. Later, when their children resumed development and began to take steps toward independence and autonomy, the parents protested, even complaining to me that analysis was changing the relationship between parent and child. However, these patients' most profound attempts to control were evident in the object-coercive doubting. I speculate that its origin was in the child's uncertainty about what was happening to his or her body and how was it taking place when, at the time of incomplete differentiation, the child's genitals were repeatedly stimulated. The child struggled against his or her intrapsychic resistance against knowing, the latter accentuated by the denial of reality by the mother.

Although colleagues have told me of similar doubting in patients who had experienced paternal incest, I myself have not seen object-coercive doubting except where the mother has sexually overstimulated the child from a time before the differentiation process normally evolves. I have seen in paternal incest patients a considerable amount of rumination about "did it occur?" but the quality of this self-doubting process is different from that of pressuring me in object-coercive doubting. I keep an open mind about this, however, and remain interested in hearing material that might corroborate object-coercive doubting in paternal incest victims. Although paternal incest is more common than maternal incest, I find it interesting that I encountered a large number of paternal incest cases only after the analysis of the first two maternal incest cases had been completed. While it would be easy to say that it is happenstance, I really have no explanation for this phenomenon in my practice. I do not rule out a countertransference reaction that could have prevented me from responding to subtle paternal incest cues. My patients' material about maternal incest was not at all subtle.

In cases of either maternal or paternal incest (I have had no patients in treatment who had been sexually molested by both parents), I found residues that persisted for many years into the analysis. These residues took the form of learning problems, as well as of "somatic memories," which were in the form of hyper- or hypoasthesia, hyperacousis, hyperosmia, and urinary, genital tract, or gastrointestinal sensations for which there was no apparent cause. I have recently reported (Kramer 1990) on these residues and welcome material from colleagues about such phenomena.

Last year, my practice included four adult patients, three in whom paternal incest and one in whom maternal incest as a child played an important part in their distorted psychological development. At the same time, a woman whose analysis I was supervising revealed that she had undergone years of frightening sexual (and emotional) abuse by her father. She was self-demeaning and masochistic, submitting to repeated painful medical procedures by third-rate physicians. She felt she could not leave these inadequate doctors, as she could not free herself from her father. She felt that she deserved nothing better.

A male whose analysis I supervised was depressed, masochistic, yet sadistically manipulative, wanting love, admiration, and salvation from other men but finding it impossible to extract them. At the same time, he revealed a tendency to relate to women very sadistically, using them as need-satisfying objects and then discarding them. His analysis revealed that he used women sexually and then rejected them, as he had been used by his mother for her sexual gratification and then had been coldly ignored. In analysis, he presented the picture of someone who, with a sense of entitlement, was an exception to usual moral and ethical rules of conduct. Being an exception was to identify with his father's habitual dishonesty. Also, it helped him extract recompense for his suffering as a child. The patient had a prostitute-like quality in that he pandered to men (emotionally, not sexually) and pleased them in order to receive their benefi-cence. Yet whatever he received in analysis or in his behavior outside of analysis was not satisfying; he wanted a strong father-like person who would stop his acting out as his father should have stopped his mother from her incestuous use of her son, and the patient from participating. His wish to be his father's favor-ite stirred up homosexual fantasies, causing him to feel as de-meaned as he had felt when he was sexually abused by his mother.

We see similar mental mechanisms in the clinical cases described by others in this volume. Two of the authors, Brandt Steele and Marvin Margolis, have already written some of the most significant papers about incest in the analytic literature. Here, they further elaborate on their astute clinical observations in two separate chapters. A third chapter is by Maurice Apprey, who, from his participation in a treatment program for pregnant adolescents, sheds light on the transgenerational sequelae of incest. He reports the phenomenological and dynamic vicissi-tudes of psychological doubting and acting out in an adolescent whose birth was the result of incest experienced by her mother. The chapters by Steele, Margolis, and Apprey are critically evaluated and discussed by Ruth Fischer, Salman Akhtar, and Hossein Etezady respectively. Following this academic dialogue, I attempt to summarize what we learn from it, as well as make some comments on my experience in the treatment of incest victims.

REFERENCES

Blos, P. (1967). The second individuation process of adolescence. *Psychoanalytic Study of the Child* 22:162–186. New York: International Universities Press.

Ferenczi, S. (1933). Confusion of tongues between the adult and the child. In *Final Contributions to the Problems and Methods of Psychoanalysis*, pp. 156–167. London: Hogarth Press, 1955.

Fischer, N. (1989). Anorexia nervosa and unresolved rapprochement conflicts: a case study. *International Journal of Psycho-Analysis* 70:41–54.

Freud, S. (1931). Female Sexuality. *Standard Edition* 21:225–243.

———— (1932). Femininity. *Standard Edition* 23:112–135.

Kluft, R., ed. (1990). *Incest-Related Syndromes of Adult Psychopathology*. Washington, DC: American Psychiatric Press.

Kramer, S., and Akhtar, S. (1988). The developmental context of internalized preoedipal object relations: clinical applications of Mahler's theory of symbiosis and separation–individuation. *Psychoanalytic Quarterly* 47:547–575.

Kramer, S. (1974). Episodes of severe ego regression in the course of adolescent analysis. In *The Analyst and the Adolescent at Work*, ed. M. Harley, pp. 190–231. New York: Quadrangle Press.

———— (1980). Residues of split-object and split-self dichotomies in adolescence. In *Rapprochement*, ed. R. Lax et al., pp. 417–438. New York: International Universities Press.

———— (1983). Object-coercive doubting: a pathological defensive response to maternal incest. In *Defense and Resistance*, ed. H. Blum, pp. 325–351. New York: International Universities Press.

———— (1990). Residues of incest. In *Adult Analysis and Childhood Sexual Abuse*, ed. H. Levine, pp. 149–170. New Jersey: The Analytic Press.

Lebovici, S. (1973). The current status of the infantile neurosis. Presented at the July panel of the Association for Child Analysis, Paris.

Loewald, H. W. (1974). Current status of the concept of infantile neurosis. *Psychoanalytic Study of the Child* 29:183–188. New Haven, CT: Yale University Press.

Mahler, M. S. (1971). A study of the separation–individuation process and its possible application to borderline phenomena in the psychoanalytic situation. *Psychoanalytic Study of the Child* 26:403–424. New Haven, CT: Yale University Press.

———— (1972). The rapprochement subphase of the separation–individuation process. *Psychoanalytic Quarterly* 41:487–503.

———— (1975). On the current status of the infantile neurosis. *Journal of the American Psychoanalytic Association* 23:327–333.

Margolis, M. (1977). A preliminary study of a case of consummated mother–child incest. *Annual of Psychoanalysis* 5:267–293. New York: International Universities Press.

——— (1984). A case of mother–child incest. *Psychoanalytic Quarterly* 53:355–385.

Parens, H. (1980). An exploration of the relations of instinctual drives and the symbiosis/separation–individuation process. *Journal of the American Psychoanalytic Association* 28:89–114.

Pine, F. (1986). Margaret S. Mahler: 1897–1985. *Psychoanalytic Quarterly* 55:493–495.

Putnam, F. W., Guroff, J., Silberman, E., Barnan, L., and Post, R. (1986). Clinical phenomenology of multiple personality disorder. *Journal of Clinical Psychiatry* 47:286–293.

Ritvo, S. (1974). The current status of the infantile neurosis. *Psychoanalytic Study of the Child* 29:159–191. New Haven, CT: Yale University Press.

Shengold, L. (1967). The effects of overstimulation: rat people. *International Journal of Psycho-Analysis* 48:403–415.

——— (1974). The metaphor of the mirror. *Journal of the American Psychoanalytic Association* 22:97–115.

Steele, B. (1970). Parental abuse in infants and small children. In *Parenthood*, ed. E. Anthony and T. Benedek, pp. 449–457. Boston: Little, Brown.

——— (1981). Long-term effects of sexual abuse in childhood. In *Sexually Abused and Their Families*, ed. P. Mrazek and C. Kempe, pp. 223–234. New York: Pergamon Press.

2

THE PSYCHOPATHOLOGY OF INCEST PARTICIPANTS

Brandt F. Steele, M.D.

From a historical perspective the psychoanalytic understanding of incest began in 1896 with Freud's "The Aetiology of Hysteria," in which he described the traumatic sexual seduction of children as the essential cause of hysterical neurosis. This was met with disbelief by his colleagues, and he himself had some hesitancy in believing that such unacceptable behavior by adults could be so frequent. In his September 21, 1897 letter to Wilhelm Fliess he said he no longer believed in his theory of neurosis and expressed his disappointment that not a single analysis had been brought to a conclusion (Masson 1985). He was also surprised that even his own father would have to be accused of being perverse, although he did not specify any reason for this accusation. On October 3, he wrote Fliess that he had discovered in his own self-analysis that early in his third year his libido toward his mother had been aroused by seeing her naked. (His use of the Latin words *matrem* and *nudam* suggests that this discovery was embarrassing to him.) On October 15, he wrote that he realized he had been in love with his mother and jealous

15

of his father. He generalized this love of mother and jealousy of father to other children and referred to the gripping power of *Oedipus Rex*. Since then, the analytic literature has been replete with descriptions of the universality of the Oedipus complex, the fantasies of incest and murder in the psychic life of children, the ubiquity of the incest barrier, and the necessity of relinquishing early incestuous attachments for healthy psychic development. The persistent belief that incest existed only in phallic-oedipal fantasy has resulted in a remarkable paucity of reports in psychoanalytic literature of actual incest. Exceptions are the excellent case studies of mother–son incest by Margolis (1977, 1984), Shengold (1980), and Silber (1979). Other brief references to actual events reinforcing the effects of fantasy have been made by Greenacre (1956), Sachs (1967), and Neu (1973). Recent voluminous literature on child abuse has shown that consummated incest is a fairly common occurrence in our own culture as well as worldwide, and there is no reason to believe it has not always been so. As far as the taboo is concerned, it seems to have applied more to recognition and talking about incest rather than to incest itself. The general public and many psychiatrists and psychoanalysts still find it difficult to believe that the barrier is broken except by psychotic or unusually depraved people.

We have failed to pay adequate attention to incest for many reasons. Among them is a tendency of incest participants to consciously avoid revealing their experiences or unconsciously repress and deny them out of shame and fear of disapproval. Because incest victims have a low self-esteem and distrust of people, they do not often seek analytic therapy, and their characteristic defenses and adaptations make it extremely difficult for them to take part in a classical analytic situation. Our own close adherence to the principle that childhood fantasies of the oedipal period are the central core of adult psychopathology and that stories of incest are not real has created problems, and so has the countertransference need to avoid the embarrassment of reactivating our own oedipal fantasies. By and large, there has been little opportunity to analyze incest survivors. Analysts have therefore continued to understand and interpret actual incest activity as essentially originating in oedipal fantasy.

The case material I present is from incest participants who have been in intensive psychoanalytic therapy for periods of a few months to several years. My purpose here is to broaden and expand our understanding of incest beyond the strict confines of the oedipal theory. I have been greatly impressed by the relevance of Margaret Mahler's work, particularly her concepts of symbiosis and separation–individuation, in elucidating the psychopathology of both child and adult involved in incest.

Although not applicable to all incestuous activities, I believe the following brief case reports show the themes of incomplete separation–individuation and the corresponding attempt to maintain or re-create some sort of close "symbiotic" interaction. The continued need for such a relationship may arise from deprivation of adequate care in early development, or just the opposite, it may result from perpetuation of close maternal care and involvement that cannot be relinquished.

FATHER–DAUGHTER INCEST

Case 1

Walter E., aged 40, a divorced, middle-class, blue-collar worker, applied for treatment ten days after his 17-year-old daughter, Mary, had told her mother that her father was having sexual relations with her. He had been interviewed by the police and expected to be charged with a felony and possibly sent to prison. His ex-wife had obtained a court order prohibiting any contact with his four children. He wept as he spoke of his love for his children and of not being able to see or talk with them. He had been divorced for two and a half years and had spent alternate weekends with the children, although their mother had often found excuses for not letting them visit. His oldest daughter, Mary, had occasionally come alone to spend the weekend at his house. He recalled five episodes of sexual contact with her over the past year. He would caress and suck her breasts and insert his finger in her vagina. On the most recent occasions they had had intercourse. In some instances, he said the sexual activity began after Mary asked him to rub her back.

In the first few sessions Walter was very sad, often crying, wanting to talk but very hesitant and embarrassed. He expressed strong feelings of guilt and shame and assumed full responsibility for his actions, although he had some feelings of anger and blame toward his ex-wife. He was much comforted by Mary's phoning him despite the court order and her reassuring him that she was not angry at him. She regretted stirring up so much family trouble and expense and wished she had handled it by herself. Apparently her reporting the incest was precipitated by her resenting her father's scolding her for two occasions of secretly spending a week with her boyfriend while telling her mother she was at her father's and telling her father she was at her mother's. Very quickly he demonstrated a strong dependent transference and was eager to continue treatment. Talking and being listened to made him feel better.

Walter grew up in abject poverty, the youngest of three sons. His father was alcoholic and never had a steady job. He had no relatives, and no one knew where he came from. Walter felt he never knew his father; rarely talked with him even when he was there. He was not violent. Mother did not drink. She worked to support the family, doing housekeeping and janitorial work at a doctor's office and a bank during the week and at a movie theater on weekends. Much of this was evening work, and from early in his life Walter went with her to help. After school he would chop wood for their potbellied stove and often scoured the nearby town dump for scrap metal to sell. For some time, except in winter, he slept in a cave-like hole he had dug out behind the house. The family was treated somewhat as social outcasts by the small-town neighbors. Walter had no friends to play with and spent a great deal of time hunting and fishing in the woods and fields, developing a lifelong love of nature and the outdoors. He had two dogs he was very attached to. They were poisoned. He was a bright boy, did reasonably well in school, and was befriended by two or three school teachers who hired him to do odd jobs.

After high school Walter earned enough money to go to trade school and became a master mechanic. He eventually established his own business. He married at 21 and was divorced sixteen years later after years of marital discord. He was a "good provider" but had trouble being close or sociable. His wife expected a great deal from him but was not very supportive. He said, "She would not even wash my clothes." She expected him to do a lot of the routine housework and accused him wrongly of infidelity. Their daughter, Mary, had felt a good deal like a Cinderella, being used by mother for menial work and for the care of her three younger siblings. She had a learning problem. Her mother called her retarded, but her father helped her with her school work. Walter sympathized with her feelings of being exploited by an uncaring mother.

Walter remained attached to his mother, often driving 150 miles to spend a weekend. He did repair work on her house and her appliances, hoping to get some sort of warmth and closeness or recognition. Usually she neglected even to thank him. Recently he told her that he had not felt much loved in childhood. She replied that he had received a lot more than she had as a child. She was a last, unwanted child who had to do chores for her older siblings and then take care of her sick mother after everyone had left home. She was quite bitter about her own deprivation.

Walter recalls being aware of parental intercourse from early childhood on. He would pull the blanket over his head to cut off sight and sound and pretend to be asleep, although he felt somewhat upset, very lonely and abandoned, and possibly disgusted. He masturbated occasionally from latency on but can recall no fantasies about people, only interest in the sexual excitement he felt in his genitals. He had a few sexual experiences with promiscuous girls before he was married. He describes being "interested in sex like everybody else" but had never felt much real tenderness or love or closeness in a sexual relationship, only a release of tension. Only rarely did he recall dreams. One he did remember was "Mary's boyfriends are going to beat me up and tear my leg off. A couple of men friends from the trade school helped me out." He could not remember ever having been beat up at any time in his life, although as he talked about his dream he was reminded of being afraid as a boy of the Indians who used to camp not far from town. His father used to trade with them and then get drunk with them. Father would tell him that he would have to be careful or the Indians would kidnap him and take him away. He had dreams during most of his life of something dangerous about to happen to him. He could not recall ever having a good dream. He reported another anxiety dream; the only content of it he could recall was that it concerned his ex-wife. He associated it to the recent troubles his wife was causing him through her legal maneuvers and her lack of understanding or caring about how he felt. There was also something about the dream that was vaguely reminiscent of his unempathic mother. He had had similar dreams many times. He was very childlike in his submissive desire to understand himself and to make sure I cared about him and would help him. At the same time he had a sense of having to do it all himself and not expect or ask for help. He had a pervasive sense of worthlessness and a willingness to accept whatever fate dealt out to him. Only after many months of work could he entertain any possibility of negative feelings toward me. Therapy was interrupted after nine months when Walter went to prison for a year. After prison, therapy resumed for another year and a half.

His basic transference to me seemed to be an attachment unrelated to gender, to a pregenital caring, protective figure who could understand his feelings and help him get through his troubles. He gradually realized how his early life had influenced his behavior and how he had never really grown up inside, since he was always seeking replacement for the early emotionally

empty environment. As his older brother recently said to him, "We each grew up alone. I didn't even know you when we grew up together." In simplest terms, Walter and his daughter Mary acted out in incest the yearning to assuage the emptiness each felt as a result of inadequate close maternal "symbiotic" care.

Case 2

I have described in detail elsewhere (Steele 1980) the case of Laura, a young woman who had sexual intercourse with her father for several years following a period of genital fondling from age 4 to 9. It was with the full knowledge of the mother, who on occasion would tell the girl to sleep with father and bring back a "five-dollar bill for Mother to buy a bottle of whisky." Both father and daughter had felt deeply deprived and rejected by the alcoholic mother and turned to each other for mutual care and comforting. Laura felt that her father was the only one who had ever loved her or that she loved. She had a deep conviction that caring involved sex, and she sexualized all her many relationships with men. She even managed to develop sexual relationships with two psychiatrists who treated her.

Case 3

Henry, a 36-year-old middle management railroad employee voluntarily reported to social services and law enforcement that he wanted help for unusual sexual behavior. He was then referred for treatment. He and his wife, Carrie, had for some time been involved with other "swingers," occasional wifeswapping, and some free-for-all hetero- and homosexual encounters. For the past two years they had involved their son, Pete, now aged 10, in sexual activities: father and son in mutual oral–genital and masturbatory activity, mother and son in genital intercourse and oral–genital interactions. The son, Pete, had begun intercourse with the daughter of family friends. Henry

had cunnilingus with this same girl, and she had had intercourse with her father and another man. The backgrounds of these people are revealing.

Henry's father had been severely physically and emotionally abused by his mother. He was alcoholic, rarely worked, and severely physically and verbally abused both Henry and a five-years-younger sister. He later joined a church, stopped drinking, and became a fundamentalist preacher, but he did not stop abusing the children and neglecting his wife. Henry's mother died when he was 12, and he was sent to live with the puritanical paternal grandmother, who verbally abused and rejected him as she had abused his father. Later, his father remarried but the stepmother kicked Henry out of the house when he was about 16. Henry and his father had little contact after that time, and his recent attempts at reconciliation had not been rewarding. He says he has always loved his father but never felt accepted by him.

Henry's mother was a practical nurse who worked part-time to help support the family. She was periodically ill due to severe bronchiectasis. She came from a very chaotic background, as one of five children of a "crazy" mother who had seven husbands, six of whom died and one who committed suicide. She had experienced incest with her father and an older brother. Henry remembers his mother as being very gentle and loving, and he and she were always very close. He also felt she counted on him for support and comfort, especially when his father was making trouble or was absent, or when she was sick with her bronchiectasis. When Henry was 7, his mother had a miscarriage; he helped her and was with her when they flushed the fetus down the toilet. Henry's father was often away. When he was about 11, Henry and his mother would get into bed together, cuddling. She was lonely and needed him. He yearned to be close to her and was sexually aroused. She would open up her legs and have him enter her. He was orgastic, but not sure of ejaculation. This happened at least four times. He recalls it being a wonderful, beautiful experience, which he has sought to recapture ever since. Subsequent intercourse with a stepsister and a cousin was not as satisfying.

Henry recalls being very curious about sex as a young boy, looking, touching, and talking with a little girl his own age, and peeking through a window and seeing parental intercourse. His mother and father were often naked around the house, and he frequently saw his mother in the shower or bathtub. He began masturbating in latency, often while looking at "skin magazines" he found in trash cans. His masturbatory fantasies at present are of being "close to a woman, each with arms around each other and then crawling up inside her and becoming one with her." He believes his fantasies in puberty were quite similar.

After two years of college, he was drafted into the navy and spent three years in Vietnam. He saw some combat and killing of men, women, and children. He had various hetero- and homosexual contacts. While stationed in Manila for a while, he was in a common-law marriage with a very helpless, needy woman but left her after she tried to kill him for his insurance.

After leaving the service, he dated and then married his present wife, Carrie, a very dependent, clinging, hypochondriacal woman. They have often been separated by her hospitalizations for emotional problems and physical complaints. Carrie had been given away as a baby by her biological parents and placed in a series of orphanages and foster homes. Finally adopted, she was sexually abused by her adoptive father and a cousin. She married to get away from home, was severely physically abused by her first husband, and then divorced him. Her present marriage has been characterized by mutual clinging, dependency, frustration, periodic disappointment, and brief separations.

Henry had what was said to be a heart attack, for which he was hospitalized for a short time. While convalescing at home he was resting on a couch. His son, Pete, age 8, who was already quite aware of parental sexual activity, came up to Henry and offered to have sex with him to help him feel better. Father acquiesced, and they began their mutual masturbatory and fellatio activities. Henry felt very much that Pete, too, needed love and attention and that sexual activity was a way to provide it in a caring way.

Henry was very childish, friendly, cheerful, dependent, and accommodating (clinic personnel described him as looking like a tail-wagging puppy as he followed me around). He was pathetically grateful for any sign of consideration and acceptance. He was also eager to gain some sort of understanding about what had happened. He was clearly ashamed and quite guilty over having damaged his son and exploited his wife. He hoped to be able to make amends. He was also puzzled and bewildered by the feeling that he had always acted in what he felt was a loving, considerate way. At first, his transference seemed to be largely a passive attachment to a nonsexual parent, hoping mostly for care and protection. Later, he vacillated between thinking of me as a sensitive, empathic, caring pregenital mother and as a non-abusive father who would show him how to grow up and be a man and a good father. Although he did on a few occasions say I was not helping him enough, he was never able to express any real anger. His self-esteem was so low that he felt he did not deserve anything good anyway.

A significant part of Henry's treatment involved working through the posttraumatic stress syndrome that had resulted from his Vietnam experience. His periodic flashbacks and nightmares of violence were associated with great feelings of helplessness and fear of destruction. He related these to his actual combat experience and also, less intensely, to memories of his father's drunken rages. No evidences of his own aggression ever became apparent, and he showed no paranoid tendency to project hostility onto others in his daily living. Most obvious was a great need for something or someone to help him feel safe.

He became aware of being very deeply identified with his mother, both in her passive, submissive helplessness and in her kindly, caring, nurturing ability. He also gained insight into his great confusion between caring and sexual activity, his desire to merge with his mother, his inability to leave her, and the futile search to find her again. There was no evidence that he had ever really mourned the death of his mother, which had occurred a year after their episodes of intercourse. His search for a spouse led to his marriage to a clinging sickly woman like his mother.

Both Henry and Walter married women who were much like their mothers. As wives, they demanded a great deal of support and help but were not able to supply what their husbands needed to repair the damages of early life. Henry's past was more chaotic and tumultuous; Walter's was uniformly bleak and empty. Henry's father was rejecting and violent; Walter's emotionally absent; both boys had little normal fathering and were left with only mothers to turn to for whatever care was available, thus increasing their dependent need for basic primary care. Although the details of their later behaviors are quite different, they continued to seek a symbiotic-like relationship. This need for a symbiotic-like relationship appeared in the transference as well as in their daily lives.

MOTHER–SON INCEST

The two most thorough reports of mother–son incest in the psychoanalytic literature are those by Margolis (1977, 1984) and Shengold (1980).

Margolis describes the nine-year therapy of John, 19, who had been arrested on his mother's complaint that he had sexually assaulted her and had threatened to kill her and her boyfriend. John was "a multiply traumatized individual in relationship with two parents who, in a very complicated way, were able to both love their son and sustain his early development while being destructive of the very growth they had nurtured" (p. 357). A brother was born fourteen months after John. After the brother's birth, John's father began to drink heavily and severely beat his wife and children. John was often exposed to parental fighting and parental intercourse. He was described as "never being a cuddly baby and not liking to be handled or kissed. Yet he was his mother's favorite" (p. 357). John took showers with his father and baths with his mother at ages 3 and 4. He was sexually aroused by her soaping his body and by the sight of her breasts and genitals. After his father went to work, John crept into bed with his mother. Despite the beatings, John had happy memories of his father and was quite attached to him. His parents began separating when John was 3, and his father left permanently when John was 6. Except for a period of several years in a Catholic home for boys, he and his brother and mother lived with a grandfather, where he slept in bed with his mother. He was attached to his grandfather and was bitter when they moved out when he was 16. In the apartment where he and mother lived they had separate bedrooms, but she continued to undress and dress in his presence.

John began masturbating at age 12 with fantasies of intercourse with his mother, and he openly expressed sexual interest in her. In a seductive way, she finally agreed to his wishes, and they continued having sexual relations about every other month for the next three years.

Dr. Margolis firmly urged both John and his mother to live separately, and both strongly resisted. John felt that his mother should spend more time caring for his needs to make up for neglect in early childhood. His mother seemed equally incapable of living independently, and after separate apartments were established, she would phone John to entice him to come back. Incest recurred in the second year of treatment when Margolis was away for two weeks. Margolis describes the transference as basically a "mother transference more characteristic of severe pregenital character disorders." At the same time, he deliberately offered himself as "a new model for identification and acted in a very fatherly way toward the patient" (pp. 276–277). The patient's original cool, distrustful, sullen, obstinate, and demanding behavior changed in therapy to become more passive, dependent, and boyish.

John had no close, intimate friends but had poor toleration of being alone. He had two marriages and was active sexually, but there was little tenderness, affection, or mutuality. There were many masochistic, self-defeating, self-destructive behaviors. He was in many ways a very moral man; he did not lie, use drugs, or drink to excess. Prohibition of aggression was more severe than against sexuality.

Margolis described John's central conflicts as "of a pregenital nature, despite the seemingly genital 'oedipal' nature of his major symptom." Coitus served as a channel for anger at a mother he experienced as rejecting and depriving. It also supported fantasies of omnipotence and wishes for closeness. He said that after he had intercourse with his mother he would often feel like "king of the world" (pp. 355–385).

After a brief five-year follow-up, Margolis (1984) wrote: "Incest is understood as a compromise formation in which most aspects of the positive oedipus are repressed, while limited direct or defensively altered expression of oedipal and pre-oedipal impulses are allowed. Super-ego development is considered as being complete, although the super-ego is pathologically malformed and is responsible for the patient's pervasive feeling of guilt and his extreme need for punishment for his incestuous behavior. These findings contradict the views of those who understand mother–son incest as representing only direct expression of positive oedipal wishes made possible by a weak deficient super-ego" (p. 355).

For three years Shengold (1980) analyzed a married man who complained of unhappiness, depression, and a difficulty in achieving success.

> While trying to fulfill his ambition to be rich and famous, he would provoke rejection and failure. He had a "good," unexciting marriage. Sexual performance was good mechanically, but with little pleasure. He was the first child of his

mother, who had wanted a girl. His mother was often depressed, and had bursts of rage and violence that terrified him. There was a smoldering war between the parents. His father was weak and passively ineffectual in response to his wife. He often absented himself by working out of town. There were periods of calm, and he felt that both parents loved him, although his father remained distant. He was his mother's favorite. Mother fed him well, was obsessed with bowel function, and frequently gave him enemas. She wiped his anus until he was of school age. She insisted on his having long hair with curls and forced him to wear outfits that resembled dresses. He believed she did this to spite the father. At age 4 he rebelled, refusing to leave the house until he got pants to wear, and at age 5 he cut off his curls. Mother seemed subtly to admire his rebellion, and he felt that she wanted him to look like a girl but not act like one. She never depreciated his genitals. She occasionally beat him, but he was more afraid of her rage than the beating. He was terrified if she had his father spank him.

Sometime after he successfully rebelled against mother, he was seduced or forced to have passive anal intercourse by an adolescent male relative his mother used as a babysitter. The youth's homosexuality was common knowledge in the family. Mother was temporarily alarmed and obsessed by the fear that her son would be oversexualized, but her alarm subsided after the anal tears had healed.

In school his prowess in sports and his good looks led girls to seek him out. He was both pleased and frightened. At puberty he masturbated with vague fantasies about girls. By age 12 he was taller than his father and both proud and ashamed of his large genitals and his erections. His mother resumed her interest in his body. He was upset by her intrusions, yet sexually excited by her. She would walk in on him in the bathroom and would look in on him in the morning as he lay in bed, uncovered, with an erection. He began to have disturbing dreams and do poorly in school. He recalled feeling angry, revengeful, anxious, and sexually excited.

One day on coming home from school he found himself, as usual, alone with his mother. She had just emerged from a bath and had left the bathroom door open. As he approached, she bent over as if to wipe her feet with a towel. She gave him a look of invitation, and again bent over, presenting another open door. He was overwhelmed with excitement, and penis erect, he advanced toward her as if in a trance. He penetrated her vagina. She had an orgasm. He was not yet capable of ejaculation but there was a kind of orgasm. It was felt as a wonderful experience. This sequence was repeated several times over the next few weeks, always without words, and it was never mutually acknowledged. Then, not long after the incestuous contact began, the boy achieved ejaculation after penetrating his mother. She noted it, became violently disturbed, and rushed away shrieking, "No, no, no." The incest was never repeated, and never subsequently mentioned. The boy apparently repressed it, and the memory reemerged only after several years of analysis. He recalled that the one-time ejaculation had been glorious, and the entire incestuous contact was remembered as wonderful and beautiful. After these repressed memories had been uncovered, the patient felt relief and liberation, but then seemed unable to integrate it further into his life. He became stubbornly resistant for a few months and left analysis.

Shengold believed that the breaking of the incest barrier between mother and son is found in the mind of the mother. In this case the mother's fear of pregnancy reestablished the barrier, and her "no, no, no" seemed to be shared by the son. They stopped the incest and never spoke of it again. Unfortunately, no further information about the mother was available. Shengold considered her to be an emotionally disturbed person, although not psychotic like incestuous mothers reported in the literature.

FATHER–SON INCEST

The sexual activity between Henry and his son, Pete, began in the midst of an already highly sexualized family relationship created by the parents. Pete approached his sick father with an offer of sex to make him feel better. Like his father, he had amalgamated sexual activity with sympathy and comforting care.

Langsley, Schwartz, and Fairbairn (1968) report in detail the case of David, a 20-year-old man who was first seen in an acute psychotic state with sexual hallucinations following his first trial of LSD. When the boy was 12 years old, his father had instituted weight lifting as a body-building exercise, which was followed by massaging each other's bodies and mutual masturbation. This continued for a year and a half, the father rationalizing his seduction as wanting his son to realize his genitals were no different than the rest of his body. This father had been raised by a mother who was sexually seductive but also verbally puritanical and antisex. He had been seduced into mutual masturbation at age 12 by a 19-year-old uncle. He was sexually inhibited in his teens; once when a girl was interested in sexual exploration, he declined. He had fantasies about both boys and girls and became enamored of an 8-year-old boy named David without any actual sexual contact. He had another mutual masturbation experience at age 25 with a male cousin and described it as his first satisfying sexual experience. He married at age 36 and named his son David after the 8-year-old David, whom he called his "first love." The marital sexual relationship was described as quite satisfactory. The mother was secretive about her life, was not open about her feelings, and took in a very matter-of-fact way the revelation of the sexual activity between her husband and son. In this case, it seemed the father was reliving his own distorted development with his son, under the guise of fatherly help in body building, thereby channeling his covert erotic interest in boys.

SOME FACTORS LEADING TO INCEST

Listening to the life stories of these people who have been involved in actual incest, one soon realizes that incest is a much more complex phenomenon than one would suspect from the psychoanalytic theory of the Oedipus complex. There is no doubt that young children have fantasies of sexual relations with parents or other primary caregivers, as well as accompanying fantasies of unpleasant consequences that lead the child to relinquish sexual fantasies and develop defenses. Even if the child could not repress the instinctually driven fantasies, could the incest barrier be broken without the cooperation or coercion of the adult? It seems unlikely that a reasonably normal adult could not resist even the most seductive sexual advances of a child. So what is it that leads adult and child into incest?

The Wish for Company

From earliest infancy there seems to be a basic need that is a special variant or quality of what we consider to be the libidinal drive. Anna Freud (1965) described it as the infant's "wish for company" (p. 155), existing along with the basic needs for food, sleep, and protection that are satisfied by the primary attachment figure, usually the mother. This "wish for company" is possibly the early form of what we loosely call the "social instinct" in mankind, which can be conceptualized as a component or derivative of Mahler's symbiotic phase of development, the necessity for the presence of another person to maintain physiological and psychological equilibrium. This "wish for company" remains with us all of our lives, probably as a continuation of the early obligatory attachment process.

Furman (1982) wrote about how "mothers have to be there to be left," referring to the experiences of separation from weaning to adolescence. I would like to add that mothers *have to have been there to be left*. If the mother has not been adequately there, the need and yearning for that kind of care persists, and the process of separation remains difficult and incomplete. Although physical and hormonal sexual development have matured, the sexual behavior in the incest participant is still deeply determined by the yearning for what is basically primary maternal care. Often, during therapy, I have heard an adult former incest victim sob in a little girl voice, "I want a mommy." Walter, while in prison, wrote to me, with some embarrassment, that he wanted to see me sometime and give me a hug and be hugged. It would be a mistake to interpret his statement as homoerotic or as an inverted Oedipus, rather than a more primitive level of a need for closeness, a "wish for company."

Symbiotic Need in Father–Daughter Incest

Many incest participants, both adult and child, speak of emptiness, lack of satisfaction, and a yearning for closeness, care, and attention. Particularly in father–daughter incest, there is the description of feeling a prolonged lack of need satisfaction from wife and mother. The girl feels that mother has never been close or really caring in any way and possibly has been actively rejecting. The father is responding to the current reality of the uncaring, rejecting attitude of his wife, but is typically also responding to feelings of deprivation rooted in his earliest childhood. The two begin sympathetically to share their deprivation feelings, progress to physically holding and comforting, and then to sexual activity. The primitive need for company has become sexualized. Rarely is there a conscious plan to be sexual at the start. Only as the relationship continues do genital sexual urges become a predominant motive.

Lack of Separation–Individuation in Mother–Son Incest

The situation in mother–son incest is almost the opposite; the close interaction between mother and child has been adequately good, but damagingly prolonged, far beyond the time for appropriate progress to separation–individuation. Mothers not only have to be there to be left, but they must also be happy and willing to see their sons develop and leave. The mothers of

Shengold's and Margolis's patients were unable to do this. They remained deeply involved in their boys' lives and from early on seductively sexualized their interactions so as to keep the boys' attention and drives excessively focused on them instead of exploring the rest of the world. Thus it seems that the occurrence of incest is less the outcome of normal development of the sexual drives and much more the result of the mother's perpetuation and sexualization of the early symbiotic phase, along with blockage of separation–individuation. Incest serves to satisfy the self-centered maternal needs at the exploitation and expense of the son's development.

The prolongation of close mother–son interactions has been described as common in Japan, where mother–son incest is apparently much more common than in our country. In a review entitled "Incest—Japanese Style," Kitahara (1989) comments on "the excessive closeness between mother and son and its consequences in Japanese culture" (p. 446), and goes on to say, "It appears that to a Japanese mother, her son is a small, dependent child forever, and she feels she must take care of him forever. Indeed, the way they teach their sons to masturbate, help them to ejaculate, and tell them how frequently they may do so, sounds like another form of toilet training" (p. 449). It is not surprising that consummated incest, largely at the mother's instigation, is a sequel of this relationship. What we would call normal separation–individuation has certainly been distorted and delayed.

Sexualized Attention

The close association of sex and loving care is not in itself abnormal. We consider it part of an ideal marriage or other committed intimate relationships. In fact, our common phrase "to make love" carries this same implication. In a less appropriate way, some adolescent males will blackmail a girlfriend by saying, "If you really loved me, you would have sex with me."

The combining of sexual stimulation with caregiving can occur very early in an infant's life.

Haynes-Seman and Krugman (1989) have described this pattern of "sexualized attention" seen in dysfunctional families as "a behavioral interaction between caregiver and preverbal child in which the adult appears to be sexually stimulated or involves the child in sexually stimulating games." For example, a father will repeatedly tickle his child's penis as part of general tickling play or have a baby bounce up and down on his lap so that the baby's feet stimulate the father's genitals. Such behavior most often occurs as part of normal caregiving attention or play. It is well known that caregivers have often used genital stimulation to distract and soothe infants and small children. In many incest participants there is vulnerability to sexualization of attention due to either deprivation or prolonged fixation at primitive levels of close interactive caring.

We see the same dynamics of sexualized attention in many situations of nonviolent pedophilia. Other dynamics, however, exist in many incest cases, especially the elements of sadism and aggression that are important in cases of dominating patriarchal fathers, rape, and the sexual misuse of infants and small children, as in prostitution and pornography.

INCEST BARRIER OR TABOO

There is apparently no universally accepted theory for the origin of the incest taboo, and it may well be that there is no single explanation for it. As for father–daughter incest, the taboo has been more against recognizing its existence than against its occurrence. The taboo against mother–son incest may well have specific origin. I have briefly seen two young men who had complaints of difficulty in feeling adequately intimate and comfortable with their wives. Sexual relations were satisfactory but accompanied by vague anxiety. Both young men were only children. Their fathers were good but possibly a bit submissive; their mothers very good and caring but always somewhat intrusive, inquisitive, and controlling. Their childhoods were in no way remarkable except for feeling that their fathers were a bit distant and that their mothers had kept too close and made independence difficult. Sex education had been inadequate or repressed. At age 13 one told his mother that he wanted to have dates and asked her to tell him what girls were like. She responded by taking him to the bedroom, partially undressing, and putting his hand on her vulva. He fled in acute anxiety and never spoke about the episode. The other young man, also at age 13, asked his mother to explain sex to him and clarify what he had heard from other boys. She explained things to him, then pulled up her dress, spread her legs, and said, "Here, I'll show you how it's done." He fled in terror. Neither of these young men expressed any sense of competition with their fathers or any suggestion of castrative retaliation. Both described a feeling of great fear of being taken over, trapped, or engulfed by the seductive mother. Coming at the time of adolescent surge toward independence, the seductive invitation to merge into the mother was panicking. No indication of homosexual trends was seen in either man; their heterosexual activity, however, was marred by their feelings of caution and hesitancy to commit fully to intimacy. The incest taboo was broken by their mothers. The barrier was maintained by the sons out of the fear of being pulled back and merged into the undifferentiated state of development. I have no idea how often this fear is the basis of the incest barrier. Certainly it would apply only to boys, and not to incest activity between fathers and daughters. In the cases of consummated incest described by Margolis and Shengold, and my case of Henry, the sons enjoyed the sexual activity with their mothers, felt it was glorious and wonderful, and were not fearful. It is possible they were still in a prolongation of elements of the symbiotic phase, not fully involved in separation–individuation, and hence not afraid of merging.

CONCLUSION

I have dealt with only a few of the human variables that combine to initiate incest, and I am aware that what I have described is not necessarily applicable to all incest participants. I believe, nevertheless, that Margaret Mahler provided us with a conceptual framework describing the necessity of a normal, symbiotic phase, and the gradual development of separation–individuation that helps us understand the origins of incest behavior in many of the patients we see.

REFERENCES

Freud, A. (1965). *Normality and Pathology in Childhood.* New York: International Universities Press.

Freud, S. (1896). The aetiology of hysteria. *Standard Edition* 3:187–221.

Furman, E. (1982). Mothers have to be there to be left. *Psychoanalytic Study of the Child* 37:15–28. New Haven, CT: Yale University Press.

Greenacre, P. (1956). Re-evaluation of the process of working through. *International Journal of Psycho-Analysis* 37:439–444.

Haynes-Seman, C., and Krugman, R. (1989). Sexualized attention: normal interaction or precursor to sexual abuse. *American Journal of Orthopsychiatry* 59:238–245.

Kitahara, M. (1989). Incest—Japanese style. *Journal of Psychohistory* 16:446–450.

Langsley, D., Schwartz, M., and Fairbairn, R. (1968). Father–son incest. *Comprehensive Psychiatry* 9:218–226.

Mahler, M., Pine, F., and Bergman, A. (1975). *The Psychological Birth of the Human Infant.* New York: Basic Books.

Margolis, M. (1977). A preliminary report of a case of consummated mother–son incest. *Annual of Psychoanalysis* 5:267–293.

——— (1984). A case of mother–adolescent son incest: follow-up study. *Psychoanaltyic Quarterly* 53:355–385.

Masson, J. M. (1985). *The Complete letters of Sigmund Freud to Wilhelm Fliess, 1887–1904.* Cambridge, MA: Harvard University Press.

Neu, J. (1973). Fantasy and memory: the aetiological role of thoughts according to Freud. *International Journal of Psycho-Analysis* 54:383–398.

Sachs, O. (1967). Distinctions between fantasy and reality elements in memory and reconstruction. *International Journal of Psycho-Analysis* 48:416–423.

Shengold, L. (1980). Some reflections on a case of mother–adolescent son incest. *International Journal of Psycho-Analysis* 61:461–476.

Silber, A. (1979). Childhood seduction, parental pathology and hysterical symptomatology: the genesis of an altered state of consciousness. *International Journal of Psycho-Analysis* 60:109–116.

Steele, B. (1980). Psychodynamic factors in child abuse. In *The Battered Child*, ed. C. H. Kempe and R. E. Helfer, pp. 49–85. Chicago: University of Chicago Press.

3

THE UNRESOLVED RAPPROCHEMENT CRISIS: AN IMPORTANT CONSTITUENT OF THE INCEST EXPERIENCE

Discussion of Steele's chapter, "The Psychopathology of Incest Participants"

Ruth M. S. Fischer, M.D.

Incest occurs. It occurs with alarming frequency. It is not merely a fantasy. But what is it that allows a parent to engage in such abuse? This is the challenge that Dr. Steele sets before us. In response, he addresses the early mother–child relationship, illustrated with clinical material from the case of Walter, a participant in father–daughter incest, and Henry, a victim of mother–son incest. Differences and similarities are noted in the two cases and it is suggested that these might be typical constellations: the mother unavailable to her daughter, leaving her yearning for closeness, which she satisfies in the relationship with the father, who is similarly deprived; and the son who is not allowed to separate.

I note more similarity than difference in the relationships these two men experienced. Neither mother was in tune with the needs of her child. One was not available; the other, also not available. Both were there for their own purposes. Both men married women like their mothers. They both experienced little fathering, whether rejecting and violent or virtually absent.

They were both left to their mothers for their total care. And they both continued to seek a symbiotic-like relationship in which they confused caring with sexuality. They both presented themselves as childlike, seeking someone to help them feel safe. In therapy they were accommodating, being unable to express anger toward the therapist.

The emphasis of this presentation is on the mother–child relationship. Incest occurs when the mother is emotionally unavailable or unable to allow her son to separate from her. But we cannot ignore the role of the father. What are we to make of a father who, unable to obtain love, caring, and sexuality from his wife, turns to his daughter rather than to another woman? Or the father who abandons his son, allowing intimacy with the mother to take place? And what are we to make of the yearning for the father that both Walter and Henry express?

I know that Dr. Steele is in full agreement that the father's role is significant, as he has written a most comprehensive chapter on abusive fathers (Steele 1982) in which he notes the extensiveness of the problem: the wide range of abusive men as well as the commonality of a poorly developed sense of identity, low self-esteem, and a sense of emptiness that they experience, along with a lack of empathy for the child's immaturity, dependency, and helplessness. These men have suffered emotional deprivation themselves, which is reflected in their poor attachment and empathy. He also writes (Steele 1982), "We rarely see abuse by one spouse that is not either consciously or unconsciously condoned and tolerated, if not actually abetted by the other spouse" (p. 489).

I am reminded here of Herzog's (1982) study of the effect of father loss due to divorce in children in the first five years of life. He describes a longing for the father who modulates drive expression, in fantasy as well as in reality. His focus is primarily on the aggressive drive, but sexual drive is considered as well. Two-year-old Ira cannot sleep as he feels unprotected from projected hostile fantasies, and Mommy's presence is not adequate to comfort him. He needs Daddy. Joey becomes aggressively destructive in nursery school, feeling he needs a big hand to punish him, and Brenda, depressed, her anger unmodulated by father, is turned inward. The role of the father as modulator of the aggressive drive was sorely missed by these children.

In addition, the father's presence is missed in the adult–adult interaction that serves to protect the child from overwhelming parent–child interaction. This is particularly relevant to the children we are discussing here. Henry's and Walter's fathers were not available to their wives and certainly not helpful to their children in terms of modulation of aggressive or libidinal drive or of overwhelming parent–child interaction. Even though physically present, they were not emotionally available to the child. It is the very absence of the father as a modulating presence that throws the child ever more forcefully under the mother's influence. Of course, the father is important in helping the child move out of the closeness with the mother, to be the important other in the separation process.

Incest is not purely a problem of mother and child. It occurs when there is a major problem in relatedness between the child and both parents. It cannot occur unless both parents participate. It is striking, therefore, that we concentrate on the mother–child relationship when what we are discussing is most commonly a breach in the father–child relationship. Certainly there is a great deal of evidence for the existence of a poor mother–child relationship in families in which father–child incest occurs. We frequently note the complicity of the mother. But it is complicity. She is not the perpetrator. It is important to understand the role that the mother plays in the incest experience. But the emphasis on mothering when we are discussing father–child incest is puzzling. In mother–child incest, the focus is on the mother. We may note the father's participation, his allowing the act to occur and recur, but the focus is on the mother. She is the perpetrator. So why not focus on the perpetrator in father–child incest?

There is a general tendency in psychiatry to blame the mother: the witch hunt, the schizophrenogenic mother, the malignant, pathogenic mother. Is there something specific about incest that focuses our attention legitimately on the mother, or is this just another manifestation of mother-blaming? When did mother become so powerful, so malignant? Traditionally, the father has been all-powerful, all-important. It was he who was at the center of the child's psychological life: the Oedipus complex, the superego, the love for, hate and fear of, competition with and for the father. These have been the cornerstones of our theory.

As we have become increasingly interested in the preoedipal period, our appreciation of the role of the mother in the child's development has been enhanced. We now take into consideration the mother of the oral, anal, and early genital phases, the mother of separation–individuation, and Kohut's (1971) idealizing, mirroring mother. Possibly this has resulted in a too great awareness of the mother's importance and has led to fear of her power. We have seen the father as the force for law and order, of conflict and growth, and of neuroses. The mother, however, is being seen as the deprivor, the cause of severe character disorder, psychosis, and, in this context, the one who allows, even promotes, sexual molestation of helpless children. In seeking to understand the psychopathology of the incest participant, we must examine our prejudices. Why has the mother become the villain? Why do we not focus on the main perpetrator of these heinous acts? Why is it that we hold the mother to be responsible? And how is it related to our new appreciation of the preoedipal years and the preoedipal parent?

This tendency to blame the mother is noted in the cases presented. Walter committed incest with his daughter. Dr. Steele (1990) tells us that "in simplest terms, Walter and his daughter Mary acted out in incest the yearning to assuage the emptiness each felt as a result of inadequate close maternal symbiotic care" (p. 8). They were both the victims of poor mothering. Walter's mother and wife were unable to care and to give. The feeling of exploitation by an uncaring mother was shared with his daughter, Mary. His mother turned to Walter and Walter turned to Mary to compensate for an unavailable, unsupportive spouse. We are also told that Walter's father was alcoholic, irresponsible, and unable to relate.

Does the father bear no responsibility for tenderness toward and care of his children? Do we mean to imply that this is purely a maternal responsibility? Are we not demonstrating a cultural bias here that interferes with our scientific objectivity? Why should the mother be the sole source of empathy, caring, and relatedness? Walter was probably as much exploited by his uncaring father as by his uncaring mother.

There is also a semantic problem since when we use the word *maternal*, we often actually refer to parental nurturance, caring, and empathy. This problem arises because in the first few years of a child's life parental nurturance has traditionally been associated with maternal care.

This problem presents itself again in the case of Laura, another victim of father–daughter incest. "Laura felt that father was the only one who ever loved her or that she loved" (Steele 1990, p. 8). She was deprived of maternal care and comfort. Was she not deprived of parental care and comfort if her father turned to her as a sexual partner rather than as a parent?

Henry sexually abused his son, Pete. He himself had engaged in sexual intercourse with his mother. As father–daughter incest is understood as a yearning for primary maternal care, mother–son incest is understood as the mother's inability to separate from the son. It is ". . . the result of the mother's perpetuation and sexualization of the early symbiotic phase, along with blockage of separation–individuation" (Steele 1990, p. 22). Although the mother is a powerful and important figure in the early years, have we not empowered her more than is justified, and have we not emasculated the father? Is the father's input in this so-called maternal care so minimal? Can we discount it so readily?

Mother-blaming, empowering the mother, and disempowering the father are noted in many of the cases in the literature. It is often seen in our patients' stories and feelings. The mother is held responsible. She did not protect her child. She allowed this to happen. In a case of father–son incest I treated, the young man, my patient, focused exclusively and for the longest time on his mother's aloofness from his father and her sons and her frequent illnesses, which allowed the father to roam the house at night seeking closeness with his sons. It was only after we were way into the treatment and after a great deal of perseverance on my part that he was able to deal with the underlying rage and despair in his feelings toward his father that had been covered by the anger at his mother.

Another patient of mine, a young woman, was sexually abused by her father when her mother underwent psychiatric hospitalization. As the oldest daughter, she took on the responsibility of running the household and all that that entailed. She, too, focused on her mother's abandonment, on her mother's setting the stage and thereby allowing this to occur. For some reason, the horror of the act committed by the father was overlooked.

In yet another case, that of a young girl who had experienced incest at the hands of her brother, the focus was on the mother, who left her in the care of the brother in spite of agonizing protestation. Another girl blamed her mother and grandmother for not protecting her stepsister from the grandfather's sexual abuse. When in adolescence, her younger brother began to molest her, the mother advised her not to be upset. Feelings toward the men—grandfather, father, brother—were all kept under wraps.

The mother is responsible. She allowed this to happen. She did not protect her child. If the mother had given more to the child and to her husband, the father would not have been tempted. Our patients, as well as our own case write-ups and theoretical discussions, reflect this.

Possibly there is some great psychological truth at the bottom of this prejudice. Maybe it reveals a remnant of our belief, a belief of patient and therapist alike, in the mother's omnipotence, and a remnant, or more than a remnant, of our fury at the disappointing mother who can never fulfill our hopes and wishes for her wonderful, protecting, infantilizing omnipotence. We are angry, disappointed, and never quite willing to accept it; never quite willing to let pass an opportunity to display our wrath. She has failed us, failed to live up to our impossible hopes and dreams, and we cannot forgive her. Or possibly we overemphasize the disappointing mother to draw our attention away from the father. We avert our eyes to protect ourselves from an even greater disappointment.

Whatever the reason for our need to focus on the pathogenic mother, if we are to understand the psychopathology of the incest participant, we must focus on the father as well as the mother. When this is done, we note, in consistent fashion, a return to the mother, this time to the poor mothering of these malignant fathers. They have had inattentive, unempathic, unavailable, self-centered mothers. But they have learned about being men from their fathers as well as from their mothers, and they have also learned from their fathers how men treat women and how adults treat children. The few studies we do have all pinpoint the same sort of fathering. Their fathers have not been available to them. They have not been empathic, understanding, or consistently present for their children or their wives. They have been violent or abusive in some ways. But these are not psychoanalyses. We need more in-depth studies to help us delineate the psychology of the participant. Possibly, through these analyses, we will also obtain a better understanding of the very striking phenomenon of ignoring the important contribution of the father to his child's nurturance.

In harking back to Herzog's (1982) studies, there is an important clue that we must follow up, which is the father's role in the modulation of the child's aggression. Incest is an act of unmodulated aggression against a helpless child. The absent father, the father who is unable to modulate his own aggression, will be unable to play the role of modulator for his child, who in turn may act against his or her own children. We must explore the father's role not only in the arena of aggression, but also in the arena of nurturance. The case examples presented in this symposium are helpful in this respect. They serve as a beginning.

We began our theoretical understanding with the father at the center: the Oedipus complex. Recently, we have expanded our horizons to include the preoedipal period and the role of the mother. We have arrived at a new juncture. Now we find ourselves in a position in which it is necessary to reinstate the father to a position of importance, only this time in the preoedipal period. We need to understand better his role in this earlier period. Suggestions are made in terms of modulation of aggression, balancing an adult–adult interaction to protect the child from overwhelming parent–child interaction, being the important other in helping the child to move out of the closeness with the mother, and the father's special contribution to the child's nurturance.

As important as it is to formulate the father's role in the incest experience as well as in the nurturing experience, it is germane to this symposium to delineate the specifics of the attachment experience, whether it is with father, mother, or, no doubt as is usually the case, with aspects of both. Dr. Steele (1982) has called incest a disorder of attachment. Today, he more specifically relates it to the symbiotic relationship and the separation experience: Anna Freud's (1965) "the wish for company" and Furman's (1982) "mothers have to be there to be left." I, like Dr. Steele, find Dr. Mahler's conceptualization of the separation–individuation experience most helpful in understanding Henry and Walter and their incestuous experiences. Contrary to

Dr. Steele, I see no need to resort to the concepts of Freud and Furman, as I find them encompassed in Mahler's theory. The fact that both Furman and A. Freud note these developmental experiences only underlines their importance.

Anna Freud's "the wish for company" is understood in Mahler's terms as an aspect of the symbiotic phase in which the other becomes important in maintaining physiological and psychological equilibrium, that is, object relations are established within the matrix of drive satisfaction. The wish for company is the result of an adequate symbiosis. This is contrasted with the ability to be alone, which is the result of an adequate separation-individuation experience with the establishment of object constancy. It is this that I believe is lacking in the two men, Henry and Walter.

Furman's "mothers have to be there to be left" is the establishment of the symbiosis out of which the child separates and individuates: the child sitting securely in the mother's lap, looking out at the world—the hatching process.

Parent–child incest is an insult to the psyche of the child victim. The specific traumatic impact will vary with the degree of immaturity of the child's ego, his constitutional endowment, the nature, extensiveness, and chronicity of the sexual act, the relatedness to the perpetrator, the relationship with the parents, the need to deny the event, the availability of other protectors, and the extensiveness of associated violence and hostility. These factors will determine the type and degree of psychopathology with which the child is left.

This presentation focuses on the symbiotic relationship and the ensuing separation. I propose, even more specifically, that the problem lies in the rapprochement subphase. This would be inevitable because of the nature of the insult. I say this because in order for a parent to commit incest, he or she would had to have been unable to supply the child with what is needed to negotiate rapprochement, which is the emotional availability to allow for resolution of the ambivalence and internalization of a positive maternal (or parental) representation. These children have been exploited by the parent, used for his or her own purposes, to the neglect of the child's needs. This indicates an absence of empathy, understanding, respect for, and protection of the child. It is the presence of just such empathy, understanding, respect, and protection that is required to enable the child to resolve the rapprochement crisis.

We have noted the importance of the establishment of the symbiosis. I do not focus on that here as I feel this was adequately established with Henry and Walter. Otherwise, they would have been unable to function as well as they did. The symbiosis is the beginning of relatedness. It is the infant investing in the mother. It is the prerequisite for future relatedness and for the infant's successful disengagement from the mother during subsequent development. It is the mother being there to be left. The mother has been, in Mahler's terms, the beacon of orientation. She has been there for the child to relieve his distress. A relationship has been established.

The individuals presented by Steele are seeking, yearning, for a specific other. This is not an indiscriminate, promiscuous wish for company, a seeking out of anyone or anything to fill the void. Their lives are not completely chaotic and impulse-ridden or apathetic and withdrawn. They have experienced an adequate symbiosis. They yearn for the mother who at one time was their beacon. They have been adequately, although no doubt not optimally, fused and differentiated, but inadequately separated and individuated. This points to the rapprochement.

At about 1½ to 2 years of age, the child experiences a surge of autonomy as the result of walking and the acquisition of representational thought. These momentous achievements lead to an increased awareness of vulnerability, of separateness and limitation, threatening self-esteem and omnipotence. The child feels helpless, alone, frustrated, and angry with his mother, who cannot restore the former state of omnipotent union. He turns to her to relieve his frustration, his anger. He needs her to be emotionally available to provide security and comfort, so that his anger will not overpower his love for her, so that he can maintain a positive image of her. This will allow him to internalize a positive maternal representation to call upon in time of need.

This is a difficult time for toddler and mother alike. The child is torn between wanting to use his newfound abilities, which leads to separateness, and wanting to undo the separation. There is inner conflict about and ambivalence toward the mother. The mother feels buffeted between the child's need for autonomy and dependence, between his love and hate for her. It requires great emotional flexibility on the mother's part. The child needs her to be there in order for the child to negotiate this phase of development successfully.

The problem is that parents who commit incest have often not received empathic caring themselves and thereby are unable to empathize with their children. They are not emotionally available or behaviorally predictable under the best of circumstances. We note in Walter his turning to his daughter when he feels isolated and lonely, his angry outburst when Mary spent time with her boyfriend, the alcoholic father he never knew, who never talked with him, his mother, who used him for her needs, and his use of this in his relationship with Mary—his appreciation of her feeling exploited by her mother while at the same time enacting the exploitation. And then there's Henry, whose father was so abusive and unpredictable. His mother was close, but not emotionally available to him. He was to be available for her. She counted on him for support, for comfort, and ultimately, for sexual gratification. He and his wife were unable to give to each other or to their children according to any but their own needs. This lack of emotional availability inevitably stems from and leads to problems in resolution of the rapprochement crisis, which leaves the child without a firm, internalized, comforting mother, without an adequate sense of self and other, and inadequately separated from inadequate parents. This is clearly demonstrated in these two case histories.

Rapprochement is resolved and object constancy attained when the maternal image has become intrapsychically available to the child because the actual mother was libidinally available for sustenance, comfort, and love. But what happens when the mother has not been available for sustenance, comfort, and love, as these mothers were not? The positive attachment is accomplished by maintaining two images: that of the good mother and the bad mother. Not only is the split image unable to fuse, it is reinforced, as this is the only way these children have to deal with their hatred. They separate out the bad, abusive, negligent, rage-evoking mother in order to maintain some sense of a good, comforting, supportive presence. This allows them to function. And it binds them to the abusing parent because they are unable to establish more separated object relations and a more individuated self. When object constancy has been attained, when the maternal representation has been invested primarily with love, the child's self-esteem is enhanced, and in his relationships he experiences affection, trust, and a capacity for empathy. The love object as well as the self is valued. But this has not happened here. The anger is too great and the love too small.

Having pinpointed the difficulty to a specific subphase of the separation–individuation process, what have we established? After all, there are any number of problems that might and do result from an inadequate resolution of the rapprochement crisis. Are we any closer to answering Dr. Steele's question, "What is it that allows incest to occur?" We have established necessary but not sufficient cause. We must look further.

Possibly a further answer lies in the rage. It is the extent of the child's anger that prevents the coalescing of the images of the good and the bad mother, that requires the maintenance of the split. The hate overcomes the love. These children experience the parental rage that is directed toward them. And they are enraged at being used and at feeling overwhelmed, helpless, and sexually overstimulated. But this rage must be denied in order to maintain the sense of the good parent. This leads to feeling

Ruth M. S. Fischer, M.D.

I am reminded of Greenson's (1968) concept of the boy's
need to disidentify with the mother. The union with her would
be too threatening to allow such ecstasy outside of psychosis.
Not only would it be fraught with castration anxiety as a result
of oedipal conflicts, even more forceful would be merger fears
with concomitant concerns of loss of masculine identity and
sense of self. It is an act burdened with all sorts of terrors that
would require a powerful force to overcome. I can imagine that
only psychosis or intense murderous rage would allow it. The
feeling of great power or ecstasy results from having overcome
such powerful terrors. This is not an ecstatic sexual union. Incest
is not wonderful. There is little love involved.

I hope I have addressed myself to Dr. Steele's challenge,
which is what allows incest to occur. I note the importance of
the rapprochement subphase, the resolution of ambivalence with
the internalization of the fused maternal image, which leads to the
development of the capacity for definitive separateness, a sense
of self, empathy, and the ability to experience modulated aggression, all of which are missing in the incest experience. The
role of the father is explored as the modulator of aggression,
sexuality, and closeness.

REFERENCES

Arlow, J. A. (1990). Psychoanalysis and the quest for morality. Paper presented at the
    Philadelphia Psychoanalytic Society Scientific session, Philadelphia, Pennsylva-
    nia.

Bachman, G., Moeller, T., and Benett, J. (1988). Childhood sexual abuse and the
    consequences in adult women. *Obstetrics and Gynecology* 71:636–638.

Bender, L., and Blau, A. (1937). The reactions of children to sexual relations with
    adults. *American Journal of Orthopsychiatry* 7:500–518.

Burland, J. A., and Raskin, R. (1990). The psychoanalysis of adults who were sexually
    abused in childhood. A preliminary report from the discussion group of the
    American Psychoanalytic Association, New York, December 1989.

Ferenczi, S. (1933). Confusion of tongues between the adult and the child. In *Final*

overwhelmingly helpless as a result of the inabil
edge the rage against the needed parent.

It is not rage alone that is an important co:
constellation that allows incest to occur, it is t
engendered by rage at the needed parent and the i
ate it—what Shengold (1979) refers to as "doubletl
murder," which leads to an apparent absence of i
have Dr. Steele's observation of the lack of the a
individuals to express anger toward the therapis
note the absence of anger and attribute it to the ne
incestuous activity secret. I believe that this is sec

Denial dictated by the environment merely i
child's inner need to deny in order to maintain soi
protecting other. The denial is of the rage as w
abuse. Here we return to the unresolved rapproch
In order to maintain a sense of a protecting othe
disappointment, and frustration need to be directe
child cannot blame the parent. He needs him, or th
much to allow this to happen. It is his only source
security, and protection. Herein lies the explanat
secretiveness, the absence of memory, the resistanc
the hypnoid states, the somatic memory, and the a
sence of anger: it is the inability to resolve the ambiv.
the resultant need to maintain the image of the spl
parent.

This also explains the puzzling fact of Henry's r
of incest with his mother as such a wondrous event th.
the rest of his life trying to recapture it. Or John, Dr.
(1977) adolescent, who felt like the "king of the world
experience of incest with his mother. The focus on th
of it all is due to the danger in experiencing the rag
would kill off the needed good object. And there was, a
concern that John might actually murder his mother.
stand the feeling of triumph as one of triumph over fe
helplessness and rage through the activity of sexual un

Contributions to the Problems and Methods of Psychoanalysis, pp. 156–167. London: Hogarth Press, 1955.

Frank, A. (1969). The unrememberable and the unforgettable: passive primal repression. *Psychoanalytic Study of the Child* 24:48–77. New York: International Universities Press.

Freud, S. (1893–1895). Studies on hysteria. *Standard Edition* 2:1–319.

Greenson, R. (1968). Disidentifying from mother. *International Journal of Psycho-Analysis* 49:370–376.

Herzog, J. M. (1982). On father hunger: the father's role in the modulation of aggressive drive and fantasy. In *Father and Child Developmental and Clinical Perspectives*, ed. S. Cath, A. Gurwitt, and J. Ross, pp. 163–173. Boston: Little, Brown.

Jacobson, E. (1954). The "exceptions": an elaboration of Freud's character study. *Psychoanalytic Study of the Child* 14:135–154. New York: International Universities Press.

Katan, A. (1973). Children who were raped. *Psychoanalytic Study of the Child* 28:208–224. New Haven, CT: Yale University Press.

Kohut, H. (1971). *The Analysis of the Self*. New York: International Universities Press.

Kramer, S. (1983). Object coercive doubting: a pathological defensive response to maternal incest. *Journal of the American Psychoanalytic Association* 31:325–351.

Kramer, S. (1990). Residues of incest. In *Adult Analysis and Childhood Sexual Abuse*, ed. H. B. Levin, pp. 149–170. Hillsdale, NJ: Analytic Press.

Mahler, M. S., Pine, F., and Bergman, A. (1975). *The Psychological Birth of the Human Infant*. New York: Basic Books.

Margolis, M. (1977). A preliminary study of a case of consummated mother–son incest. *Annual of Psychoanalysis* 5:267–293.

Margolis, M. (1984). A case of mother–adolescent son incest: a follow-up study. *Psychoanalytic Quarterly* 53:355–385.

Rascovsky, M., and Rascovsky, A. (1950). On consummated incest. *International Journal of Psycho-Analysis* 31:32–47.

Rosenfeld, A., Nadelson, C., Krieger, M., and Backman, J. (1977). Incest and sexual abuse of children. *Journal of the American Academy of Child Psychiatry* 16:327–339.

Shengold, L. (1979). Child abuse and deprivation: soul murder. *Journal of the American Psychoanalytic Association* 27:533–559.

——— (1980). Some reflections on a case of mother–son incest. *International Journal of Psycho-Analysis* 61:461–475.

——— (1989). *Soul Murder*. New Haven, CT: Yale University Press.

Silber, A. (1979). Childhood seduction, parental pathology and hysterical symptomatology: the genesis of an altered state of consciousness. *International Journal of Psycho-Analysis* 60:109–116.

Steele, B. (1970). Parental abuse of infants and small children. In *Parenthood: Its Psychology and Psychopathology*, ed. A. J. Anthony and T. Benedek, pp. 439–447. Boston: Little, Brown.

—— (1982). Abusive fathers. In *Father and Child*, ed. S. Cath, A. Gurwitt, and J. Ross, pp. 481–507. Boston: Little, Brown.

—— (1983). The effect of abuse and neglect on psychological development. In *Frontiers of Infant Psychiatry*, ed. J. Call, E. Galenson, and R. Tyson, pp. 235–244. New York: Basic Books.

—— (1984). Child abuse. In *The Reconstruction of Trauma: Its Significance in Clinical Work*, ed. A. Rothstein, pp. 59–72. Madison, CT: International Universities Press.

—— (1991). The psychopathology of incest participants. In *The Trauma of Transgression: Psychotherapy of Incest Victims*, ed. S. Kramer and S. Akhtar, pp. 13–37. Northvale, NJ: Jason Aronson.

4

PARENT–CHILD INCEST: ANALYTIC TREATMENT EXPERIENCES WITH FOLLOW-UP DATA

Marvin Margolis, M.D., Ph.D

Recognizing the pervasiveness of incest is a phenomenon of our times. It is not accidental that it coincides with acknowledging the reality of the massive trauma involved in our generation's experience of war, genocide, especially the Holocaust, and nuclear destruction. Such acknowledgment is a slow process marked by frequent collective, regressive movements toward denial and doubt. The subject of incest is painful and it is understandable that we want to turn away from studying and researching it. In the past decade psychoanalysts such as Selma Kramer (1983) and Brandt Steele (1981) have written some of the most significant papers for helping us refocus our attention on this area of inquiry. I have purposely used the word refocus, as psychoanalysts from the beginning of our field's history, including Ferenczi (1933), Freud (1939), and Abraham (1949), have cited the role of sexual trauma, especially incest or incestuous experiences, as being central to the pathogenesis of mental illness.

It would detract from the clinical focus of this chapter to trace the zigzag course of our appreciation of the significance of sexual trauma over the past few decades. Psychoanalysts have often backed off from this issue for very good reasons. We came to appreciate that the truth was hard to determine, particularly when dealing clinically with the reconstruction of the events of a person's early life. It seemed to many that it would be more scientifically sound and clinically useful to focus our attention on the information gleaned from the here-and-now clinical interaction. The understanding of conflictual fantasies as expressed in transference relationships pushed reconstruction of the past, memory recall, and even dream analysis to a more peripheral place in our clinical work.

However, even in Freud's thinking, as much as he came to emphasize the role of fantasy, there was always an appreciation of the complementary value of real events and their interaction with fantasy. This has increasingly come to be our current stance as we attempt to integrate more fully actual happenings with psychic sequelae in our theory. I would suggest that our frequent movement away from such interactive theoretical positions reflects in part our natural and understandable inclination to back away from a full immersion in the traumatic pasts of our patients. The history of our science and profession is repeated in the personal odyssey of all therapists as they grapple with these issues.

Even today with the significant upsurge of contributions to the psychoanalytic literature on incest, many in our field still report either that incest is rare in their cases or they see only the less malignant forms of this phenomenon such as parents' exposing themselves or occasional parental caressing of their children's genitalia. Apparently the more flagrant cases of incest often seek treatment from nonanalytic clinicians or else these experiences do not surface in their analytic treatment. There are several explanations for these observations. Some analysts feel that such severely traumatized individuals would not be suitable for analytic treatment. Many colleagues do not sufficiently facilitate the recall, reconstruction, and working through of the full traumatic component of their patients' past. Those analysts who have come to be interested in this clinical phenomenon report that a significant percentage of their patients have incest in their background, and that with experience, these analysts are increasingly able in psychotherapy or analysis to help their patients acknowledge and deal effectively with such events. I currently have three patients with childhood incest in their backgrounds; two are in analysis. This has been fairly typical of my practice for the past decade and none of these patients was referred to me because of my interest in incest. It may be worthwhile to note that younger colleagues seem to be more comfortable with this perspective, and in my experience, more frequently report treating such cases. I have myself supervised several candidates' successful analyses of adults who experienced incest in childhood. In the past, such cases would have been considered unsuitable for candidate analysis.

We have a need in our field for reports of such in-depth analytic experiences with the victims of childhood incest. In addition, there is a need to report follow-up experiences with such cases. This chapter discusses two such experiences. The first is that of a case of consummated mother–adolescent son incest treated in psychoanalytic psychotherapy for eight years (the psychotherapy has ranged from one–three sessions per week) with two five-year follow-ups and a subsequent additional period of psychotherapy. The second case is that of a woman who was sexually abused by her father throughout the first three years of her life. The patient was in a five-session-per-week analysis for four years.

Some of the issues emphasized in this chapter are:

1. With such severely traumatized individuals, what are the indications and possible limits of analytic-type therapy?
2. As incest always takes place within the context of other traumatic factors, for example, physical abuse, emo-

tional neglect, hunger, and so forth, can we isolate and study the sexual component as a discrete etiologic factor?

3. Are there any discernible ego-strengthening effects of the sexual trauma that would make for both adaptation and a better potential for treatment?

4. What countertransference reactions are to be expected when treating this type of patient?

5. What are the dangers in treating such patients?

6. What is the particular role of guilt in these patients' reactions to therapy?

The clinical data used to answer these questions are based largely on the treatment of the two cases presented, although in the final section a larger number of patient data is used for the evidential base upon which some tentative observations are made. From the outset I want to emphasize that any provisional conclusions are to be treated as tentative hypotheses that must await verification from a larger number of such cases.

CASE 1—JOHN BROWN

John was 19 years of age when he began psychotherapy. He had a three-year history of sexual relations with his mother prior to beginning treatment. His treatment spanned nine years. The psychotherapy was interrupted by the patient twice and finally precipitously terminated in the ninth year. By agreement, a follow-up series of interviews took place after five years. The treatment and initial follow-up have been previously reported in detail (Margolis 1977, 1984). The present report will focus on a second five-year follow-up that took place ten years after termination, and on a subsequent three-year period of psychotherapy that commenced one year after the second follow-up. Thus I have been able to follow this patient for twenty-three years since the active period of incest, which occurred when he was between the ages of 16 and 19.

The patient was initially hospitalized on the complaint of his mother after he sexually assaulted and threatened to kill her. These events occurred after he discovered her having intercourse with her date for the evening. The initial evaluation revealed a three-year history of sexual intercourse on an at least a once-every-other-month basis. After a week in the hospital, the young man began psychotherapy with me as an alternative to jail. He eventually became a voluntary patient. The history revealed a multiply traumatized individual whose parents, in a very complicated way, were able both to love their son and to sustain his early development while being destructive of the very growth they had nurtured.

The patient's premature birth was accompanied by the physician's prediction that his survival was doubtful. His subsequent survival became a family myth. He was always to remain his mother's favorite even after the birth of his only sibling, a fourteen-month-younger brother. John was not a cuddly baby, according to his mother; however, he was described as an attractive, robust child of good health and high intelligence.

John's parents were a hardworking young couple of working-class origins from an ethnic, religious background; they remained attached to their extended families, but had no close friends. John's father began drinking heavily after the patient's birth, and became physically abusive to his wife and children. The patient was subject to chronic, often disabling, anxiety due to chronic exposure to primal scene and severe beatings. John also took showers with his father and baths with his mother. He can recall being sexually aroused by his mother both by the soaping of his genitals and by looking at her breasts and genitalia. Unannounced surgery (tonsillectomy and appendectomy) when he was 4 and 5 completed John's early traumatic background.

The parents divorced when the patient was 6 years old. John, who was very attached to his father, was only to see him three times during the remainder of his childhood and adolescence despite the fact that the father lived close by in the neighborhood. The mother moved back into her parents' home and returned to full-time employment. John and his brother were placed in an orphanage for the next eight years by the mother because her elderly, sick parents said that they could not live with young children. The mother brought her sons home on alternate Sundays. While in the orphanage, John became a very obedient, studious, and responsible boy.

When John was 14, his mother was able to reestablish her own home and the boys returned to live with her. John always slept with his mother and recalls frequently being sexually aroused. Mother regularly dressed and undressed in front of the boys. John began masturbation at age 12, accompanied by frank, open incestuous fantasies. At age 16, John began to have sexual relations with his mother. They typically occurred when the mother was drunk. The patient and his mother both enjoyed and were gratified by their incestuous acts. The patient recalls lustful acts devoid of tenderness or romantic feelings. He has no recall of fantasies regarding establishing a future home or having children with his mother. Following their intercourse, the mother always castigated the patient for his "immoral" acts by saying, "You are a bum like your father." Subsequently John was remorseful for many weeks. His mother blamed him and always insisted that he had forced her to have sex with him.

The patient meanwhile continued to be an excellent student and outstanding athlete in his high school. Later on he would regard his football career as the high point of his life. John's mother encouraged his growing independence in the area of academics and athletics. However, she discouraged his social development, particularly dating, by binding him more closely to her through their shared sexual passion. The patient's movement toward individuation thus was uneven. John was not close to any friends, and only occasionally dated. He felt that this was the worst period of his life. John felt trapped and unable to extricate himself from his attraction to his mother. He felt doomed. At the time of initial evaluation, the patient had recently graduated from high school and was working; he sporadically enrolled in night courses at a local university.

John now began outpatient psychotherapy on a three-times-weekly basis. He was not a psychologically-minded individual. He often missed his appointments and slowly reduced the frequency to two times a week; in the final years he came but once a week. The patient was never fully open, he was not usually capable of free association, nor did he work much with transference.

The patient was initially wary of the treatment and kept a cool, suspicious distance for many months. Much early work was dedicated to helping him understand his distancing stance as a protection against being hurt by me or hurting me. Of necessity, much work was focused around the continuing sadomasochistic relationship of John and his mother. It became clear that the mother and son were very attached to each other, and incest still occasionally occurred. Direct advice regarding the advisability of separate living arrangements was ignored. Many months elapsed before they consented to live apart. The patient and his brother now moved out and lived together. They were close and have remained close throughout the years. The mother was now able to become more involved with her boyfriend, whom she subsequently married; it was to be a lifelong liaison.

As the sexual involvement of the incestuous couple receded, interpretative work was devoted to understanding the masochistic aspects of John's personality, especially as it was related to the profound sense of guilt he experienced as a consequence of the incest. It was clear that both the patient and his mother were rigidly moral individuals trapped in a self-destructive attraction to each other. The patient's conscience was sadistic and punitive; it was reinforced by the mother's attempt to displace her guilt onto him. She herself never entered treatment, insisting that she had been a victim of her son's lust. John readily accepted the primary responsibility for the incest. He was unconsciously enraged both by her neglectful style of mothering and her blaming him for the incest. It was several years before he could begin to accept the basically preoedipal anger he felt toward her that had been hidden by his remorseful, self-punitive character. His sexual lust was tinged with sadism and lacked the more tender, romantic features of the oedipal boy toward his mother. Guilt and castration anxiety could not be mobilized centrally in the early years of our work together. His constant preoccupation with openly incestuous fantasies slowly began to recede. It was clear that I served for some time as a supportive figure, psychologically experienced as interpositioned between his mother and himself. The last time he had intercourse with his mother was in the second year of the treatment at a time I was on vacation. Countertransference issues were prominent from the onset of this case: during the initial evaluation, in my attempt to distance myself from anyone who could have sex with his mother, I was showing concern that the patient might be psychotic. Many months elapsed before I was able to allow myself to inquire about and learn the details of the incestuous acts. It was to take several years for me to explore these issues more adequately with the patient. It must be recognized that the patient was probably never able to describe fully his mental state at the time of his incestuous experiences with his mother.

The patient slowly began to have a social life consisting primarily of sports activities with male friends and some dating; subsequently he also obtained regular employment. After three years of treatment, he had his first serious, romantic, sexual relationship. John became involved with a somewhat older, controlling, college-educated woman who belittled him for his lesser academic and occupational accomplishments. However, John was very pleased that he could perform sexually in a satisfactory manner. Despite its turbulent character, the relationship progressed; the patient now decided to terminate treatment for the first time. Some months later, when the woman threatened to break off their relationship, the patient became enraged, attacked her physically, breaking her nose, and also attempted to strangle her. He subsequently became suicidal and deeply depressed. John now refused food and drink as he had once before in his life, when his father left home. He had to be briefly hospitalized.

John now returned to psychotherapy. The couple was re-united and planned to marry. The patient was unable to reflect on the obvious dangers of such a course. Their subsequent marriage was stormy and painful. John's wife continued to deprecate him for his lack of ambition and his dependent, possessive manner. She was disloyal and unresponsive to his needs. There were frequent physical altercations. The patient quit treatment, but some months later returned when his wife filed for divorce. Again, the patient was depressed, but this time did not require hospitalization.

The patient now returned for a third period of treatment. His need to become involved in such an abusive relationship was understood in terms of his attempt to repeat and master the earlier traumatic relationship with his mother. It now also seemed clear that he was seeking his lost father, a theme that increasingly emerged as a central issue in his treatment. John began a new period of insight, growth, and development. This pattern of a self-arranged catastrophe and a return to treatment, followed by a new period of enhanced personal development, has been repeatedly observed over the course of his twenty-three years of treatment and follow-up.

During this last period of treatment, the material took on a decidedly oedipal cast and was so interpreted. John's masochistic behavior was masking and expressing, albeit in a disguised manner, strong homosexual yearnings for his father. The patient balked at accepting this interpretive trend, especially as expressed in the transference. John now obtained a position in a manufacturing plant and began to be promoted regularly. He became romantically involved with a secretary at work, who seemed to love him and who had a compatible background and life-style; he again voiced an interest in terminating. He was satisfied with what he had accomplished. John was no longer consciously troubled by sexual interest in his mother. He had friends, hobbies, and an excellent job. With an impending marriage, he decided to end his treatment. I attempted to demonstrate the link between our discussion of homosexual issues and his desire to quit, but as usual, once embarked on a course of action, John was difficult to dissuade.

I felt that his abrupt termination repeated his father's abandonment, but now was visited upon the therapist. This type of precipitate leaving also prevented John from reexperiencing the earlier painful separation from his father. It was clear to me that in no sense had we been able to work through the patient's oedipal conflicts adequately. The patient remained at risk, and I believed that he would require further treatment in the future.

Five years later, I recontacted the patient for a series of six follow-up interviews as per our agreement. Now 32, John was pleased to see me again. He proudly showed me pictures of his three children. He was content with his marriage and had continued to do well at his job, having attained the position of plant foreman (the position his father occupied years earlier). His relationship with his mother was comfortable, and in fact, she had become a doting grandmother, the most caring of all three living grandparents. She had also developed a close relationship with his wife.

As has been previously reported in outcome literature, (Pfeffer 1961, Oremland et al. 1975, Schlessinger and Robbins 1974, Norman et al. 1976) John reproduced the dynamics central to his past treatment during his follow-up interviews. However, true to his tendency to act out, he expressed his conflicts more in behavioral terms than through verbalized transference phenomenon. During the follow-up interviews, he recklessly drove the family while he was drunk and so terrified his wife and children that she threatened to leave him unless he returned to treatment. However, by the middle of the follow-up, they had reconciled and mutually decided against the need for treatment.

Subsequent interviews indicated that he still felt guilty about the incest, even though he no longer was troubled by conscious incestuous sexual urges. John still recalled intercourse with his mother as having been the best sex that he had ever had. Dream material pointed to continued yearning for his father and his need to idealize him lest his anger and hurt emerge. He now acknowledged for the first time that his mother, the incestuous parent, had been the more caring of his two parents. His dreams reflected intense oedipal anxiety and guilt. John still felt himself to be a man apart from others, marked for an early death. He recalled a recurrent dream in which he had read his own obituary. The patient recognized a need to continue working on his problems, particularly the "supermacho" characteristics that interfered with work relationships, but he decided not to resume treatment. I had concerns that the follow-up might cause regression, but a follow-up on the follow-up revealed that the patient had used the few sessions to enhance insight and was now again moving forward in his personal development. He expressed gratitude for my help in previous years, admitting that he had never dreamed that he would marry and have a family; he was more than happy about the treatment results to date.

The next contacts involved a return for a three-session consultation in 1985, which was followed by his second scheduled 1986 five-year follow-up. Three months later, in early 1987, the patient, at his own request, resumed psychotherapy, which continued for the next three years (1987–1990).

The patient presented in 1985 and 1986 with essentially the same clinical picture except that the problems had so intensified that in 1987 he opted to return to treatment. John was now in his late thirties. He had become the plant manager and had also been assigned many important staff tasks of a highly technical nature. For example, he was given the job of overseeing the building of a new plant complete with very high-tech equipment. This type of project would ordinarily require technical overseeing by an engineer. Meanwhile, the company had gradually grown to a firm with multimillion dollars in sales. Being a plant manager now required upgrading of skills in accounting, inventory control, and use of computerization. John's job called for the skills of a college graduate, if not those with an MBA. Our autodidact read at night and managed to handle successfully his increasingly burdensome, stressful, and daunting assignments, all the while complaining of increased work hours, incompetent subordinates, and lack of appreciation by his bosses.

John reported that mounting anxiety and pressure frequently immobilized him, and he became confused and unable to think clearly. He would sit in his office and stare off into space. I raised questions about his obvious need for assistants and need to delegate some of his work assignments. The patient stubbornly insisted that no one else could be entrusted to properly carry out his managerial responsibilities. During this period, his health suffered: he again developed an ulcer, and had frequent upper respiratory infections. He drank excessively and smoked. Finally he requested an assistant; the owners readily agreed. He selected a woman who was to prove to be so incompetent that she simply became another part of his stressful, ever-growing work overload.

John was finally able to carry out his multiple assignments successfully and felt especially proud of shepherding the new plant from blueprint to production. Now John was often euphoric and cocky. He reduced his appointments to two times a month and began to think of terminating the present period of psychotherapy. There was much material at this time linking his company with the orphanage. In both situations, he was the devoted, responsible son who committed his full energy to the good of the institution, which in turn provided a structure for him within which he could grow secure. As the patient began to recall his days in the orphanage, he was moved to revisit it for the first time in his life. He expressed his gratitude to the nuns for their devoted help, and made a financial contribution to the school. His salary and bonuses continued to rise and he now moved to a home in a new suburban development with lake privileges. He became active in the lake association and his interest in improving community affairs soon led to his being elected president of the lake association. John was particularly interested in developing special programs for the neighborhood children.

John did not neglect the home front. He was an active, involved father, whether he was helping the children with their homework, taking them hunting and fishing, or teaching them sports skills. His world revolved around work and home. He had two friends, one of whom died during this period. John remained, as always, close to his younger brother, mother, and several other relatives. With all this activity, he also had time for avocational pursuits such as shortwave radio, raising tropical fish, and frequent hunting and fishing trips. Despite the fact that he was an expert marksman, he continued his dismal record of having shot and killed only one deer, which had occurred ten years ago, again reflecting his inordinate fear of murderous impulses.

Approaching the summer of 1989, the patient's condition suddenly began to deteriorate. John was informed that the owners had decided to sell the plant, and he felt personally betrayed. He was now alternately enraged and saddened, and at times he acted as if he had been stunned by a severe blow and rendered immobile. John was convinced that he would not be retained by the new owners in such a responsible position, given his lack of academic and professional credentials. John now felt that his years of loyal, devoted service had been for naught. He had a second source of painful conflict. After many months of training, he decided that his assistant was incompetent and reluctantly recommended her discharge. His boss readily agreed. The employee subsequently came crying to John and begged not to be dismissed; he now fell into an obsessional state about his decision. He wondered whether or not he had been fair to her, and helped her enough, and given her enough time to learn their procedures. John became agitated, depressed, and nonfunctional. Again, the patient was beyond my interpretative reach and I could not help him. It was akin to watching a Greek tragedy unfold.

Unfortunately, at this time I left for my summer vacation. Since I would be abroad and moving around frequently, I gave the patient the name of a colleague to call if an emergency should develop. Upon my return, I was notified by John's wife that during my absence he had become even more depressed, and had requested a leave of absence from work. Moreover, he did not call the covering psychiatrist, but upon the urging of his distraught wife, accepted a referral by their family physician to a local psychotherapist for medication and religion-oriented counseling. As the patient was out of town, I left a message that I had returned and would now be available to meet with him. I was very concerned, as John had never sought out other therapists. Since I had not heard from him one week later, I called, and discovered that the patient had made a serious suicide attempt upon his return from vacation and had been hospitalized. I immediately established telephone contact with the patient and his psychiatrist. The patient was in a very deep depression and near obsessional delirium. He was still ruminating about the decision to fire his assistant and was extremely self-condemnatory about this action. John regressed further during the hospital stay, sinking into a state in which he did not want to see his family or even to go back to his job. He obsessed about the possibility of moving to northern Michigan to start a new life as owner and manager of a supply store for fishermen and tourists. He even considered leaving his family behind and never seeing them again.

John remained in the hospital for three weeks. Upon his release, he resumed psychotherapy with me, at first on a daily basis, which was subsequently reduced to three times a week when he felt ready to return to work. After a few weeks, he felt that his improvement would allow a further reduction to twice-a-week appointments. Because he drove two and a half hours round-trip for each appointment, he has always used this as a reason to limit the frequency of his treatment.

In reviewing his state of mind when he made the suicide attempt, John recalled that he drank a fifth of bourbon while ingesting a bottle of antidepressant pills given to him by his new therapist. He remembered talking out loud to his workaholic friend, Joe, who had died of a massive heart attack, and who had given him the liquor on the patient's birthday, "You're right, Joe, the work did get me." We were later to understand the suicide as a masochistic expression of an underlying incestuous fantasy of reunion with his dead father. As he began to lose consciousness, he called his wife at work and she contacted the police, who took him to the hospital. On arrival, he was in a coma and required heroic resuscitation procedures. The admitting physician said that had John arrived five to ten minutes later, he would not have survived.

Our posthospitalization sessions focused on clarifying the reasons for the extreme depressive state into which he had fallen. The cause of his obsessional indecision now became clear. His assistant, truly incompetent, had nevertheless attributed her difficulties to John's perfectionistic supervisory style. He totally accepted her version just as years ago he had accepted the sole responsibility for incestuous acts with his mother. John could no more criticize his assistant than he could express his anger toward his mother for her role in their sexual relationship. The patient's anger about feeling betrayed by his boss was also rechanneled into depressive affect. My unavailability was an added issue at this time and recalled to mind being abandoned in childhood by his father.

His boss visited John in the hospital many times and despite the patient's many months of low-functioning or nonfunctioning during the summer, offered him a less stressful work assignment without any change in pay. The boss reiterated his appreciation of the patient's devotion, loyalty, and valuable performance record. Now, for the first time in the treatment, the patient acknowledged to me that he had been experiencing difficulty in carrying out the supervisory aspects of his position. John was perfectionistic and overcritical, and did not listen to his subordinates. His rough, authoritarian approach was "my way or the highway." His assistant, indeed, was incompetent and was finally fired, but the patient was also relieved of all supervisory functions. It became clear to the patient and me that his work overload was in large part due to John's inability to involve his staff in sharing certain responsibilities and instead attempting to do it all himself. His new assignment was to a relatively low-pressure staff job involving inventory control, analyses of shipping costs, and other management support functions. The reassignment, if permanent, had probably put a cap on his career in this company. He stubbornly resisted my attempts to analyze further the psychic underpinnings of his macho style of supervision as well as any efforts to understand his exaggerated sense of responsibility. There was clinical evidence to suggest that his perfectionistic supervisory style and masochistic work pattern represented the patient's attempt to deal with persistent guilt stemming from his incestuous past.

For many months, his self-confidence was low and he again complained that he knew that he was different from other people, that there was "something wrong with me." John was disturbed by an awareness of his continuing vulnerability. He wondered why his younger brother, who had not been involved in incestuous acts, was not as psychologically impaired and had a blander, happier existence. He also observed that his brother had not achieved as much as he in the professional area. It became clearer during these discussions that their mother had always preferred John to his brother and had preferentially encouraged John to succeed academically. In fact, the patient admitted that his achievements were accomplished in part with the goal to please his mother by meeting her expectations. His mother now spontaneously stated to John that she felt responsible for involving him in incestuous experiences in childhood, which she believed lay at the root of his present troubles. She asked his forgiveness. His brother, together with his wife and mother, remained close to John and were very supportive throughout these difficult times. The postsuicide-attempt treatment experience allowed John both to work more reasonable hours and become closer to his wife and children. It is important to note that the patient, over the years, has slowly assumed a more psychologically introspective stance in his own treatment. He was no longer as dismissive of my interpretations as he was in the first decade of his treatment.

During the pre- and posthospitalization period, the patient's sleep was disturbed by many dreams of sexual liaisons with women or dreams in which he was dying. Associations to women usually led to women who had been seductive, deceitful, and linked with his mother. Concerns regarding castration were reflected in frequent references to bodily damage or malfunctioning. The death theme often led to associations to his overweight condition, elevated cholesterol, and excessive drinking and smoking. Conflicts about oedipal issues were still clearly central to his psychological functioning. Death had always been a frequent theme in his treatment hours. It is as if he were doomed to death at birth, then miraculously saved, but still had a death sentence on his head. The special conditions surrounding his birth and subsequent survival, particularly his mother's central role in nursing him to health, led to a special bond between mother and son. From infancy, John was allowed special intimacies with his mother. Had these experiences inexorably led him to the conclusion that he could also allow himself the full sexual love of his mother? Would it then follow that having early on repeatedly traversed the incest taboo, John still felt that his punishment inevitably must be castration and death? Edith Jacobson (1954) in her essay "The Exceptions" posits just such an outcome in such cases: "This dangerous masochistic need for punishment seemed to be present in all the varieties of exceptions which I had an opportunity to observe" (p. 13a).

John remains, then, as a variant of the Oedipus myth, even if of less heroic proportions. Like Oedipus, he experienced abandonment and neglect. He was taken in by others to be raised and educated. With his father out of the way, he returned home to become involved in an incestuous relationship with his mother that almost led to a violent fatal outcome. Psychotherapeutic intervention, however, has allowed both patient and mother to survive and gradually approach a more normal life. In fact, each period of therapy, typically precipitated by a personal crisis, has led to a higher level of functioning and achievement. A further period of growth and development cannot be ruled out. Perhaps in this case John's early experience provided him with a uniquely circumscribed type of optimism that propels him forward from success to success. There are no closed borders; he can try anything and succeed.

John remains in a stable marriage with a reasonably happy family life. His occupational situation is again stable, but his underlying conflicts do not allow him either contentment or fulfillment. John is a guilt-ridden man, who cannot freely use his creative energies and talents; for example, he can neither complete college nor, apparently, advance further in management. He is a crippled man from the psychological standpoint, who remains highly vulnerable to the normal ups and downs of life. The patient's recent suicide attempt is ominous and reminds us that his vulnerability may still be of a life-threatening nature. Unfortunately, he cannot fully utilize an analytic treatment situation to explore and resolve his oedipal conflicts—perhaps because in full consciousness he actualized these tabooed wishes earlier in his life.

In the summer of 1990, the patient again decided to break off his treatment. He obviously was again reasonably symptom-free and content with his life. He did not want to explore further his psychological conflicts even at the limited intensity of once-a-week psychotherapy. As was his usual custom, John quit precipitously, explaining that he had used up his insurance benefits for psychiatric treatment. He felt that he was no longer so perfectionistic and that he had much less pressure at work. He no longer worked excessive overtime hours or took work home. He is proud of his new assertiveness at work in regard to assuming fewer responsibilities. His evenings and weekends are

now devoted to family activities and personal pursuits. John
appears to be more content and happy with his lot than ever
before in his life. A new president had been hired to fill the job
to which the patient had once aspired, but John showed no
apparent anger or even jealousy. He enjoyed his current highly
technical staff position. After twenty-three years of observation,
however, it remains clear that he will probably require intermittent periods of therapy throughout his life in order to maintain
his mental equilibrium.

　　While I hope to conduct a follow-up on this case in another
five years, it can never be certain that this will come to pass.
Perhaps, then, a few final observations of a more general nature
are indicated. With the passage of time, the question of how
mother–son incest can occur does not seem to be such a remarkable event in need of an explanation. Two decades ago there
were few references in the literature to this phenomenon (parent–child incest). Today, new case reports appear regularly.
This is heartening evidence of our field's ability to confront such
disturbing clinical issues. It seems clear that many clinical situations can lead to the final, common pathway of parent–child
incest; the clinical outcomes are similarly variable. The mother's
willingness to become involved in an incestuous relationship
with her son seems increasingly important as a single factor. The
incestuous inclinations of a child can easily lead to traversing the
incest taboo when the parent is encouraging of such activity.

　　This case report reflects the patient's potential for growth
through treatment despite the obvious limitations that will probably persist throughout John's life. He seems content, and yet he
is not happy about his need always to remain a secondary figure
in a support position in his company. I fear that his psychological
limitations will never allow him deep love and friendship. However, this is not to say that his narcissistic problems are central,
so I will abide by the diagnostic formulations described in my
last publication (Margolis 1984). John's diagnosis remains in the
realm of severe neurosis, complicated by pregenital charactero-

logical features. I continue to believe that my earlier diagnosis of borderline state was too severe. Oedipal conflicts remain the core of his psychic life. The extent of traumatic experiences in his childhood and adolescence will probably continue to predispose John to a dangerous degree of regression. Sadomasochistic tendencies are major features of this clinical picture. Why some individuals with this background seek a perverse solution rather than outright incest is not so clear. The clinical behavioral outcomes of incest and perversion are different and should not be confused. This topic deserves a more complete discussion, which would be beyond the bounds of this report.

CASE 2—MRS. MARTHA STONE

The following case of father-daughter incest was treated in analysis for four years. While the two cases differ in many fundamental ways, they also illustrate some common features that may be fairly typical for this clinical group.

> Mrs. Stone, a 55-year-old nursing supervisor, was referred initially for psychotherapy, which might possibly lead to analysis. She was inconsolably depressed about her marriage and had been crying intermittently for many weeks. Her three children were married and living in various parts of the country. Her alcoholic husband, a very successful physician, was deeply involved in his work and spent little time with her. Her life had been centered around her children. Now that they were grown and out of the house, she was facing an empty marriage and a dwindling social life due to her husband's drinking. She reluctantly admitted a sexual involvement of many years' duration with a previous therapist; this had ended about ten years before she began treatment with me.
>
> Mrs. Stone had been adopted at age 3 and was now considering meeting her biological brothers and sisters, who had recently contacted her requesting an opportunity to meet. They

had not seen her since she was 3. She recalled nothing about her first three years of life. Nor did she know anything about it— other than she was the youngest sibling and that she had one older sister and two older brothers. They had contacted her from time to time by letter, but she had declined to meet or talk with them. She reported having had a recurrent obsessional thought for many years that she knew something, but that if she told what is was, no one would believe it. Early recurrent dreams of a bizarre, erotic nature, together with this historical material, led to my raising a question about possible childhood sexual abuse. She had been discouraged by her previous therapist from contacting her family of origin. While her adoptive parents were caring, she had never felt that she belonged anywhere; her friendships and her marriage were not intimate. She and her husband had not had sexual relations for the past ten years. I began psychotherapy with her because of my concerns about her capacity to tolerate analysis; I left the door open to the consideration of beginning an analysis at a later time.

The patient decided to contact her family. She felt an immediate intimacy as they resumed a family life together. They had all been adopted after the deaths of their mother and father. The were all now married and two were also in the medical professions. She discovered that they had much in common, from physical similarities to verbal mannerisms. She had been their youngest sister and they had always wanted to recontact her, but they had waited until she might be ready. She decided to ask her brothers and sisters about the possibility of childhood sexual abuse. At first they insisted that she had not been sexually abused, but slowly, over many months, they began to admit to a common childhood of sexual and physical abuse by their father, who had himself been sexually abused as a child; their compliant, dying mother was aware of the incest, but did nothing to stop it.

Upon the death of the mother, the father even installed the older sister in his bed. The patient had slept and continued to sleep in a crib in the same bedroom. She had apparently been sexually abused from approximately 10 months to 3 years of age. Her siblings had made an agreement never to tell her, but had succumbed to the persistent questioning of Mrs. Stone, who, like Oedipus, wanted to know the truth. Actually, the entire story took over two years to emerge fully from their memories and be shared. The patient, because of her tender age (15 months) at the time of her mother's death and because of the concomitant sexual abuse during this period, may have endured the most trauma of all the siblings. The reunion was a very emotional time, but it seemed to bring them together and had a healing effect. All had been or were currently in treatment and had led lives of desperation and sorrow. The other siblings had been adopted by two families when the children were in their pubertal years. The children, other than the patient, resumed contact with one another in their late teen years and had since had close relationships with one another. As their mother's illness progressed to an inevitable fatal outcome, it became clear that this group of siblings had increasingly functioned as an inner family within their nuclear family, supporting one another emotionally when their mother's death left them completely at the mercy of their alcoholic, often unemployed, abusive father. It recalls to mind stories of "family" units of children that formed in concentration camps which were able to provide support and even sustenance under the worst imaginable circumstances.

The complementary collective working-through of this family horror together with the work of the analysis proved to be very useful to the patient. She found out, for example, that the obsessive thought that no one would ever believe her probably had its origin in their father's oft-repeated warnings to them never to tell anyone of the family's incestuous secret or he would kill them. These threats were accompanied by hyperreligious strictures. The horror of this family's life finally culminated in the father impregnating his oldest teenage daughter. The baby was born at home and apparently killed by the father. Protective Services were alerted by school authorities; the children were removed from the family home and the father was jailed. Subsequently, the children were adopted and the father died within the year. The disclosure of the facts of Mrs. Stone's early years, however full of tragedy, were helpful to her, as it enabled her to understand in the analysis the connection between the events of these early years and her subsequent development.

Early in the first year of the treatment, an analysis was begun. The preparatory period of psychotherapy was apparently necessary to establish her trust that I would not respond sexually to her as had happened with her previous "analytic" therapist. In this particular case, the patient was able to free-associate, to work with transference and dreams, and to allow a significant degree of controlled regression in the analytic situation. Her strengths probably derived from several sources: (1) she was emotionally and physically cared for in her early years by her teenaged sister and brothers, and (2) her adoptive parents were caring and nurturing, and she grew up within a fairly normal family from the age of 3. I hope to demonstrate that some of her strengths may, in fact, have also been derived from the very traumatic experiences of her early years.

This patient had been placed in a good family that decided not to tell her anything about her past. In fact, she was removed from the orphanage without an opportunity to say goodbye to her siblings, who were profoundly disturbed by her sudden disappearance. She subsequently became a dutiful, pleasant, high-achieving child, who was the apple of her adoptive father's eye; he preferred her to his natural children. The patient was constantly to out-perform them in school, and later became the only college graduate among them. The patient traces her excessive need to please to these early years, especially directed toward her father. She claims, for example, that her primary reason for obtaining a college education was to please her father. They shared a mutual fantasy that following her graduation they would establish a joint business undertaking. It may be that the desire to please originated in her early years with her first father; certainly, she later felt that she submitted to sexual advances by her first therapist in order to please him. Throughout her school years, she could not allow any close friendships to develop, although she had some at-arms-length relationships. She had no romantic or sexual relationships until she met and married a man she met toward the end of her college years. She cared for him, but neither did she love him nor he love her.

In the analysis, she presented as an articulate, bright, and willful lady who related to the treatment, particularly in the early months, as if it were a college assignment. On the surface, she often appeared to be cheerful, spunky, and optimistic. She wanted to learn something useful in every hour. At the onset, she was tolerant of my inability to be able to provide her with new insights in every hour, and soon she was reading books on analysis that convinced her that she was finally undergoing a real analysis and would have to be more patient. She was very goal-directed, well organized and self-reliant; one could see why this idealistic, compulsively organized woman had been so successful in her nursing career.

Meanwhile, she was often coquettish, and talked a great deal about erotic thoughts involving me, though typically, sensual depth did not accompany these thoughts. I noticed that I was often overwhelmed by the enormous number of thoughts, dreams, and "insights" she brought to our sessions. I found myself at times becoming irritated, bored, and lapsing into silence. Sometimes she had a particularly irritating way of asking me at the end of such a silent hour, "Well, what does the good doctor make of the hour today?" I interpreted her barrage as an attempt to overstimulate me and make me feel just as helpless and despairing as she had felt in her early life and during her last treatment. I also repeatedly noted how controlling and distant she was in the hour; I had the impression of a closed, sealed train traveling through a country (the analysis) without any real contact with the native inhabitants (the analyst). It became clear that this character armor had been necessary to enable her to deal with the massive trauma of her early years. Her sister, for example, painfully recalled one day finding the patient, at the age of 10 months, lying in her crib. Their father had just left the patient bleeding in the vaginal area and with semen in her mouth. Her sister said that the patient seemed not to be breathing and was apparently in a state of shock. The sister quickly carried her to the bathtub and immersed her in cold water. The patient then revived and resumed normal breathing.

Mrs. Stone had managed to remain married to a man who was basically indifferent to her, but she had not allowed herself to become fully aware of his coldness. She related more to her children, and this was the one area in which she allowed herself to have warm relations. Her optimistic, can-do attitude led her always to hope for improvement, if not happiness, in the marriage even after the couple's mechanical lovemaking ceased and her husband had further withdrawn from her into alcoholism.

The analytic work enabled the patient to begin slowly to dare to have more open relations with her students, her children, and her grandchildren. She became increasingly unhappy in her marriage as her husband's drinking increased and he became more detached from her. After long and careful consideration in the analysis, she decided on a divorce. She attributed her immediate and persistant feeling of improvement to not living with someone who ignored her.

The loosening of her defenses did not at all occur in any dramatic way. It was slow, inching work that was difficult for both of us. Her assertiveness, sexuality, and sometimes sadistic indifference were now becoming more prominent. I felt alternately excluded much of the time and intruded upon in a sometimes shocking manner. Once, at a community outreach program regularly sponsored by the Psychoanalytic Institute, she sat in an area of the auditorium where I always sat. I came late just as the program began and sat down among some friends, inadvertently sitting in the seat next to my patient. I was not consciously aware of her presence. The next day she asked me if I was. When she discovered I wasn't, she commented teasingly that I must be shocked to learn of this occurrence. Needless to say, we spent many hours coming back again and again to this incident, which made me aware that I had learned to isolate myself from involvement with the patient. I came to understand this as both self-protective and retaliatory. She admitted that she had a sudden deep, vaginal orgasm while sitting next to me, which shocked and upset her. She had not had such orgasms during her married life or during masturbation. It had only occurred once before, during a dream while she was in the analysis.

The patient began to express more robust anger in the treatment, which I knew was only the tip of the iceberg. She became increasingly critical of my lapses in technique or clinical interventions. She even began to consider registering an ethical complaint against her previous therapist. A series of life-threatening events ensued that attested to the depth of the sadomasochistic currents in her personality. One night while visiting in another city, she was walking near her hotel in a dangerous area. She was robbed, and resisting, was severely beaten and slashed by her assailant. On another occasion, she was speeding on an icy highway and had a near-fatal accident that was averted at the last moment by the quick thinking of another driver. These incidents were out of character for this normally circumspect, conservative, careful nurse. Needless to say, I was alarmed by the nature and extent of this degree of acting out, and attempted to help the patient work with these issues more directly in the transference.

Perhaps my most difficult moments came when she began to express her deep, aching sadness about her past life and its missed opportunities. She despaired of ever having a real loving relationship. She bitterly lamented her decision to undertake an analysis; she had never before consciously realized how empty and sad her life was. At such times, I began to doubt the wisdom of having attempted to analyze such a traumatized patient. Had I done more harm than good? I often had doubts of the veracity of the family's history of sexual abuse; obsessional doubting, as noted by Kramer (1983), is not confined to these patients, but can also assail their therapists. The patient grieved over her traumatic, bleak childhood and her subsequent calm but anemic life. Like other cases of this type, she has always been ready to assume the responsibility for her "failures," including whatever the analysis has not yet allowed her to achieve. In fact, as she recalled the many long years of her previous treatment, she remembered having always believed that the treatment's failure, including even her inability to enjoy sex with her therapist, was her fault. She felt hopeless and believed herself to be incurable. For those who might wonder why such patients do not complain or question such abusive treatment, this patient had a plaintive reply, "I was only concerned that he not abandon me." Such patients, reexperiencing their traumatic pasts, poignantly portray the helpless state of the abused child.

The analysis continued. It was now very stormy, engaged, and mutative. It had always been a most challenging and now became a very personal treatment. The incident in the auditorium (when I hadn't realized I was sitting next to her) proved to be a turning point in the treatment, as I became even more aware of the nature and depth of my own countertransference.

In the beginning of the fifth year of the analysis, the patient retired and decided to move to the southwest to live closer to her children and grandchildren. Her personal physician also recommended the move in view of a chronic debilitating asthmatic condition. The patient would not accept my suggestion that she was leaving Michigan because of issues that had arisen in her treatment. She said that she would continue her analysis in her new place of residence. Her termination with me took place several years ago and she did continue her analysis. This clinical report of Mrs. Stone is not as complete as that of John. Space constraints have only allowed me to focus attention on certain aspects of this case; for example, I wanted to demonstrate that analysis is possible with some victims of childhood incest, and to elaborate on the role of countertransference.

While analysis is possible in some of these cases, it is not the treatment of choice for many others of the severely traumatized type. I know, however, that many of the understandings and behavioral changes that occurred in this case could only have occurred as the result of an analytic treatment. I am not certain if this patient's analysis will ever continue to a successful termination; however, she has determination, courage, and dedication to the analysis, which in itself is a hopeful sign.

Mrs. Stone was satisfied that the analysis had helped make more sense of her life—she always wondered why she didn't feel that she belonged anywhere. At the time of termination with me, she was not as anxious and depressed so much of the time as she was when she began her treatment. She had hope, and now felt that she had a more secure place in her new/old family, with her children and grandchildren and in a widening circle of new friends and interests. Now when she had feelings, whether they were happy or sad, she experienced them more deeply. This pleased her very much. She had a fantasy about termination in which she would not come for her last session and would never contact me again. She could agree that the fantasy expressed a final wish to enact revenge for her multiple abandonments. She wondered teasingly about my reaction to such a situation. Thus, it can be seen that her childhood trauma cast a long shadow over the entire course of her analysis, including the last hour.

CONCLUSION

These two cases demonstrate the impossibility of isolating the specific effects of childhood incest on the adult personality. Parent–child incest of the type described here does not occur in isolation and is accompanied by other traumatic aspects of childhood, for example, emotional neglect, physical abuse, even the effects of hunger. Perhaps recognition of the multivariate etiology of clinical outcome is a less tidy proposition, but it appears to be the more reasonable conclusion. Are there clinical observations in depth that would indicate any other possibility than that incest occurs in a traumatic context of parental sadism, abuse, and neglect? This is not to deny that because in cases of incest we are dealing with a phenomenon that encompasses a variety of clinical situations of greater or lesser degree, diagnostic outcomes can vary, but usually they do involve major psychopathology. It remains wishful thinking, perhaps due to residual oedipal fantasies, that we would expect otherwise.[1]

Psychoanalysis has a role to play in certain of these cases (Shengold 1980) and can inform our psychotherapeutic treatment of other cases. Such treatment may be intermittent or decades-long (Silber 1979) or even lifelong, but demonstrably remains worthwhile. Many colleagues unknowingly have cases with incest in their backgrounds, but do not recognize the hints that patients provide that would allow reconstruction or memory recall with subsequent integration of such material into the analytic work. The enlivening of transference would be one major consequence. When the subject of incest is avoided in our clinical work, we repeat for the patient the collusion of the nonincestuous parent who does not want to acknowledge the spouse's incestuous activity. Those colleagues who become more experienced in recognizing and facilitating their patients' need to face this part of their past soon find other cases of this type in their practice. This would particularly be true for less severe forms of parent–child and sibling incest than are reported in this chapter. Incest is probably not rare or infrequent in the backgrounds of patients who appear in our private offices requesting either psychoanalysis or psychoanalytic psychotherapy. Certainly, we have long been aware that incest looms large as a background factor in the patients who come for help in our community clinics and hospital outpatient clinics. My clinical experience leads me to the conclusion that incest appears frequently and regularly in patient groups of all socioeconomic, religious, ethnic, and racial groups.

Countertransference phenomena are ubiquitous in such cases, and clearly are often the major limiting factors that

------

1. Several reports in the literature, Yorukoglu and Kemph (1966) and Barry and Johnson (1958), minimize the ill effects of parent–child incest, but these studies are based on very meager clinical data.

prevent us from both detecting and treating such patients. Countertransference reactions are often of greater magnitude than ordinarily encountered, and involve an added risk and burden for the therapist. Availability of consultation and, of course, personal analysis would be helpful, perhaps even necessary for therapists who become involved in the treatment of such cases. Certainly, a personal analysis would be essential for the therapist involved in psychoanalytic psychotherapy or psychoanalysis with such patients.

There may be severe limits to the results we might expect in such cases. For example, we may not be able to work through the phallic-oedipal material to the extent that is ordinarily possible. One can, however, look forward to the major gains that are the consequences of treatment, which these despairing patients never dreamed of achieving. Incest is a particular behavior that crosses over into tabooed experiences that are highly conflictual. It is a reality that like other major trauma, for example, death camp experiences, incest can never fade in one's mind as a minor factor in the past. The experience of incest leaves patients vulnerable to persistent guilt and anxiety of major proportions. However, a nihilistic therapeutic stance is unwarranted by the evidence of a wide range of treatable cases that I and other analysts or psychotherapists have treated. Major limitations in treatment outcome of all cases are common, and we have come to view this as part of a more realistic appraisal of our clinical efforts.

In the course of the patient's need to repeat the original trauma, death, illness, suicide, and injuries are to be expected as major preoccupations or eventualities in such cases. Unfortunately, patients can retraumatize themselves and further aggravate their psychic wounds. The patient's life may also be at stake in such clinical situations, and the therapist must be especially attentive to such possibilities.

Trauma may lead to strengthening effects on personality development (Shengold 1980). Major trauma may lead to major strengths as well as major vulnerabilities. The incestuous child often outperforms his nonincestuous sibling. Such traits as self-reliance, dependability, ambition, optimism, persistence, devotion, idealism, and a sense of responsibility may all be associated with early sexual trauma. They are derived from successful attempts by the incest victims to survive, often primarily by their own efforts, in an abusive environment.

Some incestuous parents, paradoxically, may be the more caring parent and the mainstay of the family. In fact, the incest victim's most positive characteristics, for example, lifelong pursuit of education, are often fostered directly by the incestuous parent.

The traumatic effect of parent–child incest may be mitigated by a host of variables: support from the incestuous parent, siblings, teachers, neighbors, and others. In the cases presented here we have noted how the orphanage and the sibling group constituted such supportive factors.

Pathological guilt leading to intense sadomasochistic phenomena is often induced in the incestuous child by the hypermoralistic adult abuser. It is incorrect, therefore, to consider incestuous parents and children as grossly immoral. In fact, it is the troubled conscience of such parents that accounts for their typical hypermoralistic stance. It is also the painful conscience of the victim that so often results in lifelong masochistic excesses.

A sense of doom, a feeling of not belonging, and even a conviction that there is some unalterable deficit in one's personality are often noted in adults who have experienced incest with a parent. This may not only be related to oedipal guilt, but may also be a function of an actual, perceived awareness of a limited capacity to be intimate and loving that stems from having parents who were not able to love well. A sense of underlying rage, however buried, may contribute to the feeling of such patients that they are deviant and unworthy.

Patients who have experienced child–parent incest are psychological "exceptions" and may be understood further in terms of the "psychology of the exception" (Jacobson 1954). They have had forbidden sexual experiences as well as other special favors. Their feeling of entitlement is reinforced by their reaction to a history of neglect and abuse. Perhaps because of the forbidden pleasures they were allowed, they characteristically manifest an excessive need for punishment, which often leads to masochistic excesses, even, at times, to death.

In the case of John, he was not adversely affected by the two five-year follow-up experiences; on the contrary, he seemed to use these experiences in the interest of further growth and development. Such experiences are not without risk in terms of major acting out, but the benefits may far outweigh the risks, which can usually be managed, especially if anticipated.

The preceding observations must be considered very tentative and based on limited clinical observations. More case studies (with follow-up when possible) and more controlled research are necessary to arrive at more definitive conclusions.

REFERENCES

Abraham, K. (1949). The experiencing of sexual trauma as a form of sexual activity. In *Selected Papers of Karl Abraham*, pp. 47–63. London: The Hogarth Press.

Barry, M. J., Jr., and Johnson, A. M. (1958). The incest barrier. *Psychoanalytic Quarterly* 27:485–500.

Ferenczi, S. (1933). On the confusion of tongues between adults and the child. *Selected Papers* 3:156–167. New York: Basic Books, 1955.

Freud, S. (1939). Moses and monotheism. *Standard Edition* 23:73–75.

Jacobson, E. (1954). The "exceptions." An elaboration of Freud's character study. *Psychoanalytic Study of Child* 14:135–154. New York: International Universities Press.

Kramer, S. (1983). Object-coercive doubting: a pathological defensive response to maternal incest. *Journal of the American Psychoanalytic Association* 31:325–351.

Margolis, M. (1977). A preliminary report of a case of consummated mother–son incest. *Annual of Psychoanalysis* 5:267–293.

———— (1984). A case of mother–adolescent son incest: a follow-up study. *Psychoanalytic Quarterly* 53:355–385.

Norman, H. F., Blacker, K. H., Oremland, J. D., and Barrett, W. G. (1976). The fate of the transference neurosis after termination of satisfactory analysis. *Journal of the American Psychoanalytic Association* 24:471–498.

Oremland, J. D., Blacker, K. H., and Norman, H. F. (1975). Incompleteness in "successful" psychoanalyses: a follow-up study. *Journal of the American Psychoanalytic Association* 23:819–844.

Pfeffer, A. Z. (1961). Follow-up study of a satisfactory analysis. *Journal of the American Psychoanalytic Association* 9:698–718.

Schlessinger, N., and Robbins, F. (1974). Assessment and follow-up in psychoanalysis. *Journal of the American Psychoanalytic Association* 22:542–567.

Shengold, L. (1980). Some reflections on a case of mother–adolescent son incest. *International Journal of Psycho-Analysis* 61:461–476.

Silber, A. (1979). Childhood seduction, parental pathology and hysterical symptomatology: the genesis of an altered state of consciousness. *International Journal of Psycho-Analysis* 60:109–116.

Steele, B. F., and Alexander, H. (1981). Long-term effects of sexual abuse in childhood. In *Sexually Abused Children and their Families*, ed. P. Mrazek, and C. Kempe, pp. 223–234. Oxford, England: Pergamon Press.

Yorukoglu, A., and Kemph, J. P. (1966). Children not severely damaged by incest with a parent. *Journal of the American Academy of Child Psychiatry* 5:111–124.

5

COMPLEXITIES IN THE ETIOLOGY AND TREATMENT OF INCEST-RELATED PSYCHOPATHOLOGY

Discussion of Margolis's chapter, "Parent–Child Incest: Analytic Treatment Experiences with Follow-Up Data"

Salman Akhtar, M.D.

$\mathbf{D}$r. Margolis's chapter covers five areas: (1) some general comments on the phenomenon of incest, (2) a case of consummated mother–son incest, (3) a case of a middle-aged woman sexually abused by her father during infancy, (4) comparison of the two cases, and (5) some comments on the treatment of such cases. I will refer to each of these areas separately.

GENERAL COMMENTS ON INCEST

Dr. Margolis makes the following observations regarding incest in particular and childhood sexual abuse in general.

1. Current psychoanalytic interest in incest should be regarded as a refocusing on the phenomenon. Psychoanalysts from the beginning have cited the role of sexual trauma, especially incestuous experiences, as being central to the pathogenesis of mental illness.

2. There has been a "zigzag course" in our recognizing fully the role of actual sexual trauma in pathogenesis. However, the fact remains that Freud (1939), as much as he came to emphasize the role of oedipal fantasy, always recognized the potential of actual sexual seduction in the past.

3. Referral artifacts as well as technical limitations (arising from theoretical biases or countertransference blind spots) may make actual incest appear rare in analytic practices.

4. Incest usually occurs in the setting of multiple traumas (emotional deprivation, physical abuse, parental alcoholism, etc.). This makes it difficult to isolate its uniquely pathogenetic effect.

5. Participation of both parents is essential for parent–child incest to occur. One parent is the perpetrator of incest. The other by silence or absence unwittingly colludes with the former.

6. The incestuous parent may, at times, be the healthier of the two parents. Indeed, the positive personality traits of the incest victim may also come from interaction and identification with this parent.

7. On the one hand, incest leads to profoundly deleterious effects, including lifelong guilt, sadomasochistic tendencies, a vague but persistent dread of disaster, and vulnerability to accidents, injuries, and even suicide. On the other hand, a certain self-reliance, ambition, dogged pursuit of knowledge, and perseverance can also be traits associated with early sexual trauma.

I think the points made by Dr. Margolis are valid, theoretically sound, and clinically relevant. I am also confident that his omission of certain other areas (e.g., reasons for incest taboo, cross-cultural variations, correlation of incest with traditional psychiatric diagnoses, etc.) is to maintain focus on intrapsychic matters. There are, however, two general areas I would like to discuss. The first refers to the spectrum of severity and the second to the relationship between incest and perversion.

The spectrum of increasing psychopathology involving incest has five nodal points: (1) dormant unconscious incestuous fantasy, (2) unconscious incestuous fantasy with "continuous pressure in the direction of the conscious" (Freud 1915, p. 151) to warrant defensive operations, resulting in neurotic symptoms or displaced or disguised acting out, (3) conscious incestuous fantasy devoid of pleasurable affects and sensations, as is sometimes seen in obsessional neuroses, (4) conscious incestuous fantasy that is enjoyable and accompanied by masturbation, (5) incestuous sexual acts that increasingly come closer to the performance of genital sexual intercourse and performed with relatives of increasing physical closeness. On one end of this continuum is the ubiquitous, unconscious incestuous fantasy that is either sufficiently mourned or adequately repressed, but in both cases, behaviorally irrelevant. On the other end is heterosexual, genital orgastic intercourse with the opposite sex parent. (Sex with the mother is at the greater extreme of psychopathology than is sex with the father.)

Many factors determine an individual's location on this continuum. These include, among others, constitutional predisposition, preoedipal trauma leading to much unneutralized aggression and nonrenunciation of infantile omnipotence, a grossly distorted oedipal experience, repeated primal scene exposure, actual sexual abuse in childhood, and fostering identification with aggressor and proclivity for repetition. While it is generally not possible to tease out such contributing factors, I wish Dr. Margolis had said something about this continuum and its determinants. Why, for instance, can some people live with incestuous fantasies and others act them out in displacements, while still others are compelled to do the "real thing"?

The second issue refers to the conceptual relationship between incest and perversion (Akhtar 1991). In classical theory, the basic aim of perversion is to deny anatomical differences between sexes and therefore to reduce castration anxiety. Its other functions may include controlling aggression, enhancing body image, dehumanizing powerful objects, bridging gaps in the sense of reality, reducing separation anxiety, and alleviating depressive affects. These functions, however, are regarded as secondary; relief from castration anxiety is primary. In this theory, fetishism is the paradigmatic perversion. On the other hand, some recent psychoanalytic writings (e.g., Chasseguet-Smirgel 1984) suggest that perversion is an attempt at bypassing the father's rule, idealizing oneself instead of the father, breaking all filial links, negating generational (not anatomical) differences, returning to the mother's body unimpeded by the father's fertile penis, and, in this backward journey, creating an upside-down "anal universe" in which pregenitality is deemed superior to genitality. The main purpose of perversion here is to negate the narcissistic injury caused by the child's smallness vis-à-vis his parents' bigness. Such conceptualization leads one to assume that incest is the paradigmatic perversion.

THE CASE OF MOTHER–SON INCEST

Dr. Margolis's case report is outstanding for many reasons. First, it is one of the very few psychoanalytically oriented case reports of consummated mother–son incest. Second, it is the most detailed of such case reports. Third, the length of follow-up is striking. Such long follow-up permits an observation not only of the psychotherapy outcome but also of the patient's handling of life's newer challenges and developmental tasks. Fourth, there is a follow-up on the follow-up, thus providing an opportunity to see the effects of follow-up interviews themselves. Fifth, the style of writing is clear, elegant, and concise. And finally, Dr. Margolis's report, by demonstrating his humane commitment over the years as well as the patient's efforts at grappling with his conflicts, offers hope in an area often relegated to therapeutic nihilism.

Still, I find it difficult to discuss this case report. First of all, I have never seen such a case and must rely on experience with related cases. Second, Dr. Margolis's (1977, 1984) two previous reports on this case, together with the material in his chapter, provides too much data for me to be able to comment upon the case here. The situation is made more complex by the fact Dr. Margolis has not included a summarizing psychodynamic formulation as he did in the 1977 and 1984 reports. So you see my dilemma. If I stay exclusively with the chapter here, I might raise questions that have been answered earlier by Dr. Margolis. But if I refer to earlier reports, I run the risk of baffling readers who are unfamiliar with them. Also, to which of the two reports do I refer, as the 1977 and 1984 formulations are quite different? And is it not possible that Dr. Margolis may have further modified his views since he last published them in 1984? My solution to these dilemmas is to be extremely selective, quote from both of Dr. Margolis's formulations, raise questions about the reasons for the change in his views, and to point out certain areas that I feel have not received adequate attention in either of the three reports.

In 1977, Dr. Margolis viewed the patient as a "borderline" (p. 287) and felt that his

> . . . central conflicts are of pregenital nature, despite the seemingly genital, "oedipal" nature of his major symptom. Coitus has served as his channel for anger and resentment at a mother whom he experienced as being rejecting and depriving. Sexual relations with his mother have also supported fantasies of omnipotence and possibly also have served to sustain wishes for closeness. [p. 282]

In a later section of the same paper, six factors were identified as leading to the patient's aberrant behavior: (1) an excessively seductive mother, (2) an absent father, (3) lack of a sustained affectionate relationship with the father, (4) identification with the father's impulsivity and assaultive brutality, (5) sadism toward the mother for rejection and betrayals, and (6) feeling an "exception" (Freud 1916, Jacobson 1954, Kramer 1987), that is, one who is not subject to conventional morality, including the incest taboo. This attitude was furthered in the patient by his mother, who greatly indulged him and repeatedly made him aware of the "miraculous survival" surrounding his birth. Dr. Margolis (1977) described the patient's superego as ill developed and uneven, his defenses as primitive, his affects as shallow, and his object relations as impaired. The "major determinant of his incestuous behavior was his wish to ultimately destroy both his mother and his self" (pp. 284–285).

The follow-up data and a reconsideration of his original notes led Dr. Margolis to a different psychodynamic formulation in 1984. He changed the patient's diagnosis from borderline to "a severely disturbed neurotic" (p. 373). More important, he changed his dynamic understanding of the patient's incestuous acts. Dr. Margolis now felt that the patient had been very attached to his father during his early years and that his mother, while seductive, was not rejecting and neglectful. The patient's world

> . . . began to unravel during his oedipal years (age 3 to 6) and became a maelstrom of sexual passions and murderous intentions, primarily because of the influence of parental violence and sexual overstimulation. . . . The father's frequent absence from the family now left [the patient] with an extra burden—the added anxiety and guilt of an oedipal triumph. The phallic-oedipal period was the locus of [his] major conflicts. A defensive regression to preoedipal points of fixation now occurred, particularly focusing on the person of his mother. The patient thus presented himself in treatment as a victim of preoedipal maternal neglect. [pp. 372–373]

Actually "there was no deficiency of castration anxiety or oedipal guilt in the clinical material" (p. 373). Each act of incestuous transgression was followed by weeks of profound guilt and penance. This, coupled with the patient's otherwise rigid morality, suggested that his superego was not deficient— simply malformed and defensively compromised. The patient's sexual relationship with his mother was a complex compromise formation in which preoedipal rage was gratified, and some aspects of the Oedipus complex were manifested and others had undergone "selective repression" (p. 374). Vengeful, sadistic lust toward his mother was manifest, romantic tenderness and procreative interest were not. Negative oedipal trends and hostile competitiveness involving his father were also repressed.

> In fact, it was the repression of major aspects of positive oedipal drive that made it possible for the incest to occur without a complete psychological violation of incest taboo, i.e., the positive oedipal fantasy was not allowed full expression in the act of incest. [p. 384]

Clearly, the 1984 formulation is quite different from that given in 1977. The shifts are (1) in the diagnostic realm: from borderline to neurotic, (2) in the pathogenic realm: from a neglectful but seductive mother and absent father to a caring but seductive mother and a loved and sorely missed father, (3) in the psychostructural realm: from a superego "still in a state of formation" to a pathologic but completely developed superego, and (4) in the psychodynamic realm: from explaining the incest as the result of the patient's "wish to ultimately destroy both his mother and his self" (1977, pp. 284–285) to a complex, multilayered compromise formation that includes manifestation of some positive oedipal and mostly preoedipal wishes and repression of other positive oedipal and negative oedipal wishes.

I would not quibble about the change in diagnostic labels; nor am I tempted to take the expected oedipal–preoedipal debate route. The diagnostic labels involve a largely semantic issue; to regard what is borderline as sharply delineated from what is neurotic is in any event questionable. The same, by and large, applies to the preoedipal–oedipal debate. These things are not neatly separable; they do not exist as either/or. In fact

> . . . we are always in the world of "both/and." We deal constantly, and in turn, both with the oedipal where there is a coherent self, and the preoedipal, where there may not yet be; with defensive regressions and with developmental arrests; with defensive transferences and defensive resistances and with recreations of earlier traumatic and traumatized states. [Wallerstein 1983, p. 31]

Therefore, it makes perfect sense that both oedipal and preoedipal factors would have led this patient to have sex with his mother. The same holds true for his other experiences. For instance, feeling like he was the "king of the world" (1984, p. 360) after sex with his mother may refer not only to oedipal triumph but also to a resurgence of practicing phase hypomania (Mahler et al. 1971) after a live escape from a profound symbiotic regression. Similarly, the recurrent dream of reading his own obituary may contain not only a guilty seeking of death (castration) for his oedipal transgression but also the infantile megalomania of achieving the truly impossible. After all, he is alive while the obituary says he died during the previous year!

By not including these potential other meanings, Dr. Margolis appears to overemphasize the oedipal dimension, especially in his 1984 formulation. Still, the question is not whether it is oedipal or preoedipal. The more important questions are (1) to what extent the 1977 to 1984 shift reflects theoretical reformulation as against nine years of dedicated therapeutic work. In other words, did the borderline become neurotic because of correcting an earlier misdiagnosis or as a result of treatment by an outstanding clinician? And (2) to what extent would this patient, as a child, have been capable of intrapsychically experiencing the triadic conflict of the oedipal phase? Did he have the adequate developmental background, the psychostructural attributes for entry into a genuine oedipal phase? His lack of identity consolidation clearly speaks against it. We have an individual who does not trust people yet cannot tolerate being alone, is boyish and passive yet "living on the razor's edge of violence" (1977, p. 282), is shy and inhibited yet vigorously active in team sports, for example, football, baseball, and hockey, has shallow affects yet frequently becomes suicidally depressed and homicidally enraged, and is "obedient," "conforming," and "rigidly moral" (1984, pp. 359, 376) yet able to transgress the strictest human prohibition of all. Such contradictions are evidence of severe identity diffusion (Akhtar 1984, Kernberg 1967, 1980) and thus betray a borderline personality organization. Does such organization permit a true oedipal experience to begin with?

Stronger doubt is cast upon the patient's capacities in this regard by a careful look at the first twenty-four months of his life, which include (1) a premature birth with its associated problems, for example, maternal anxiety, perhaps a neonatal stay in the hospital in an incubator, and the effects of all this upon a comfortable entry into the symbiotic phase, (2) declaration by physicians that he would die, and later his "miraculous survival," (3) not being a "cuddly baby" and whatever that reflected constitutionally and in terms of symbiotic bonding, (4) at age 5 months, his mother's becoming pregnant, (5) at age 14 months, the birth of a sibling, and his mother's prolonged hospitalization, and (6) at age 21 months, his mother's becoming pregnant again. All this before the patient was 2 years old! Now, does this developmental background appear to be one that would lead to self- and object-constancy, the renunciation of infantile omnipotence, the capacity to mourn, the delay of gratification, and the binding of instinctual tensions through fantasy, that is, the capacities that would ordinarily be required to experience a genuinely triadic, oedipal conflict? My answer is, "not really," and I believe that suggesting otherwise is treating the patient as an "exception" even to the customary psychoanalytic theory!

Clearly, there is much more I could say about this case, but I will restrict myself to one last comment, which pertains to a specific admonition by the patient's mother. After having sex with him, she would castigate him for "being a bum like your father." On surface this is a criticism, but as being like one's father is always music to a son's ear, it also carries hidden praise! This "double-talk" (Litin et al. 1956) and "selectively permissive" (Kramer 1983) superego is typical of mothers who enact incestuous impulses with their children and give rise to "superego lacunae" (Johnson and Szurek 1952) in them.

THE CASE OF FATHER–DAUGHTER INCEST

Dr. Margolis's second case shows the cardinal characteristics of individuals traumatized by childhood incest. These include low self-esteem, denial of dependency needs through exaggerated self-reliance, vulnerability to exploitation by others, inhibited sexuality, sadomasochistic tendencies, and bouts of inconsolable sadness and despair. This patient also showed the peculiarly inviting characterological impenetrability that frequently results from traumatic bodily intrusions in childhood. And she displayed the typical tendency to be always ready to assume the responsibility for her failures. This phenomenon of an abused or severely deprived child letting the traumatizing parents off the hook (because of his or her dependence upon them and also because of a self-centered cognition) and taking the blame upon him- or herself has been observed by many psychoanalysts. Shengold (1989) has repeatedly noted it in his severely neglected or abused patients—those who have undergone "soul murder."

Fairbairn's (1944) "moral defense" and Kilingmo's (1989) "secondary intentionality" are other concepts that address this matter from varying perspectives.

The background of Dr. Margolis's patient is also typical. It confirms that parent–child incest usually occurs in a multiply traumatizing setting. Her father was violent and alcoholic. Her mother was sickly and died when the patient was only 15 months old. The patient had much primal scene exposure. She was physically abused and sexually molested by her father. She was put in an orphanage at age 3 or so and then abruptly separated from that setting (and her siblings), too. Dr. Margolis is correct in pointing out if despite these horrifying first few years of life, the patient was able to salvage considerable psychic equilibrium, it is largely because of the older siblings' care of her and later the security and warmth provided by the loving adoptive family. It was through such mitigation of early trauma that this patient acquired the capacity to consolidate a vocational identity, marry, have children, and establish a household of her own.

However, there are evidences that the inner wound was still there, alive and throbbing. Perhaps the outer adjustment was a "false self" (Winnicott 1964) or an "as-if" (Deutsch 1942) adaptation to which those abused as children are often condemned for their entire lives (Shengold 1989). Underlying her competence was chaos, which sought containment, redress, and redirection. Her adoptive father's preference of her over his own children might have reflected not only the patient's intellectual industriousness, but also her need and capacity to evoke loving rescue as well as extraordinary indulgence. In other words, underneath the calm exterior the patient was, had to be, truly provocative. This tendency was later tragically misunderstood and exploited by a therapist who started having sex with her. It also appeared in the early phases of her treatment with Dr. Margolis, who at times felt helplessly overstimulated by her. The episode of her sitting next to him at a public function showed most dramatically her need to turn the tables, to stir someone else up as she had been stirred up a long time ago. However, in all this there is also a second agenda—the communicative value of acting out. It is as if the patient were saying, "Look at what I am doing, see what my behavior is trying to tell you, decipher it, help me understand it, help me control it, help me give it up!"

Now, the observation of the communicative value of patients' actual behavior started of course from Freud's (1914) "repeating, remembering and working through" paper; yet a common temptation is to focus on the resistance aspects of acting out rather than what such behaviors reveal. (Clearly, an optimal analytic technique maintains a balanced view.) Even more frequently overlooked is the communicative (therefore adaptive) value of manifest neurotic symptoms. In this patient's case the recurrent obsessional thought that she knew something but if she told, no one would believe it, drew her and Dr. Margolis's attention to the childhood sexual abuse.

It is worthwhile to pause here and compare this recurrent thought with the phenomenon of the "object-coercive doubting" described by Kramer (1983), a unique type of doubting in which those sexually abused by mothers "coerced the maternal object or her substitute to argue one of the opposing sides of the child's intrapsychic conflict" (p. 331). These conflicts are usually about knowing something, and they never achieve a satisfactory closure. Kramer distinguished this doubting from that of the obsessive-compulsive individual. The object-coercive doubting suggests a lack of self-object differentiation, while the compulsive has separated and individuated and is torn by conflict between components of the patient's own psychic structure. On the surface, Dr. Margolis's patient appears to belong to the compulsive category. After all, she had the doubt herself and was not forcing anyone else to prove otherwise to her. Yet a closer look reveals that telling *others* and *their* not believing was a significant component of her seemingly self-contained doubt. It is as if a superficial neurotic-like layer hid a deeper lack of self-object differentiation. This reminds one that the infantile neurosis is itself at times a false-self organization, a phenomenon that has been commented upon by many British psychoanalysts (Fairbairn 1952, Guntrip 1969, Khan 1971) and hinted at in Kohut's (1971) formulations of various complex relationships between narcissistic and oedipal organizations. This brings me to the treatment issues in such cases, but before commenting upon them I will briefly compare Dr. Margolis's two cases.

COMPARISON OF THE TWO CASES

The two patients described by Dr. Margolis have many similarities. Both have a background of multiple traumas, including emotional neglect, physical abuse, and sexual overstimulation. Both had parents with severe psychopathology. As adults, both suffered from low self-esteem, chronic guilt, sadomasochistic tendencies, inappropriate marital choices, depressive mood swings, and a strange proclivity toward occasional recklessness, despite an otherwise conforming personality. However, there are important psychostructural distinctions in the two individuals, perhaps a result of one major difference in their early lives. While both were severely abused till age 3, the male patient stayed in that traumatizing situation, while the female patient was placed soon afterward in an affectionate adoptive family. As a result, she had an opportunity for healthier identifications and a different kind of latency and adolescence. This caused "softening" even of those malevolent introjects that were the legacy of her brutally traumatized infancy. A restrained persona gradually developed and masked the vague torment of early abuse. More important, the supportive relationship with her adoptive parents renewed her capacity for trust and therefore contributed to her analyzability.

Surely then, all parent–child incest does not lead to similar consequences. And if this is true, then one might legitimately

look for key factors regarding psychic structure, psychodynam-
ics, phenomenology, and transference developments that govern
differences in outcomes among incest victims. Such factors exist
perhaps in both the environment and the child. Among the first
group of factors is the degree of overall chaos in home, parental
violence and alcoholism, frequency of abuse, degree of dependence upon the abusing parent, and the availability of nonparen-
tal supportive figures. Among the second group are three important variables.

The first is whether the child is preverbal or verbal. The
absence of language (to codify, record, and subsequently recall)
alongside the ill-consolidated self-object differentiation of the
preverbal child, would render the incestuous sexual appearance
a relatively nonspecific trauma. Such traumatic overstimulation
may further impede separation–individuation (see Blum's 1979
views on preoedipal primal scene experiences in this regard) and
thus affect the later, phallic-oedipal developments. The effects
of this trauma may last all one's life as "somatic memories"
(Kramer 1990) or as an "unrememberable and unforgettable"
(Frank 1969) inner torment (with or without secondary fantasy
elaborations).

The second variable is temporally overlapping but concep-
tually quite different. It refers to whether the child is preoedipal
or oedipal. In other words, a parent's actual seduction of a child
may lead to different consequences depending upon whether or
not oedipal fantasies exist concurrently in the child. If they do
not, the child's later self-blame largely results from taking on
the responsibility of parental actions. However, if such fantasies
are active in the child when incest occurs, then a core of
"primary intentionality" (Kilingmo 1989) is also present in his
or her subsequent guilt about the incest. Though these differences are very difficult to tease out years later during analysis,
they might occasionally guide analytic interpretation and lead to
different reconstructions.

The third variable involves capacity for orgasm, which may be present in adolescents but is dubious in younger children. Since the psychosexual organization in the latter is not capable of adequate discharge of sexual tension in orgasm, the

> . . . wish for, need for, discharge is expressed through the child's fainting or sometimes by a loss of sphincter control (usually urethral) but a full release cannot be achieved. . . . [This] wish for discharge can be transformed into a wish for a passive, penetrative experience, explosive or implosive—perhaps a kind of anal orgasm. . . . [The latter] wish for an explosive penetration, even a castrative penetration, can be mobilized to end the torment of prolonged and finally unbearable forepleasure. [Shengold 1989, p. 61]

Two caveats seem warranted here. First, these three variables do not exhaust the intrinsic factors that may affect the outcome of parent–child incest; however, they do seem to be the most important ones. Second, it is not my intent to dichotomize clinical phenomena along these lines. In real life, such variables function only as friendly guideposts, not as inviolable categories. Nonetheless, keeping them in mind might help us look for, listen to, and empathize with various consequences of parent–child incest as they emerge during the treatment of such cases.

TREATMENT ISSUES

Dr. Margolis makes three extremely important points regarding the treatment of such cases. These pertain to their treatability by analytic means, countertransference reactions, and the kind of therapeutic results one may expect with them.

Treatability. Some parent–child incest victims might undergo relatively unmodified psychoanalysis. Others are often treatable with psychoanalytic psychotherapy. While such treatments may be intermittent and at times decades long, the effort remains worthwhile. Too nihilistic a stance is thus unwarranted.

Countertransference. Incest victims provoke strong emotional reactions in others. This may lead to their nonacceptance in analytic modes of treatment. Worse, they might be accepted for treatment, but the analyst's own emotions may prevent his deciphering the patient's hints regarding such a trauma in the past. This is most unfortunate, since when we avoid dealing with this background issue, we repeat for the patient the collusion of the nonincestuous parent who does not want to hear or deal with the spouse's incestuous activity. Dr. Margolis emphasizes that these patients evoke countertransference reactions of "greater magnitude than ordinarily encountered" and that this may become an added risk and burden for the therapist.

I agree with what Dr. Margolis has to say here, but will add only that the countertransference reactions themselves might have great informative potential, perhaps even more so in cases where traumatic events (sexual or otherwise) have occurred in the preverbal period. Sometimes unusual feelings, impulses, or visual images experienced by the analyst may constitute the first hint of such a trauma in the patient. A case of my own comes to mind. During the first year or so of a patient's treatment, I would often have a visual image in which a little baby was pierced by a long spear. Bleeding and still attached to the end of the spear, the baby spun helplessly. I felt no strong emotions with this image, just a vague puzzlement and curiosity. Only after some self-reflection was I able to sense in me the presence of much anxiety about this image. Still later, I could feel (alternately) both the tragic pleading, as it were, of the infant and the triumphant sadism of whoever held the spear (not a part of the image). It was, however, a long time afterward that the patient began talking of intense, ruthless, guilt-ridden impulses of stimulating children's genitalia until they were bleeding and squirming with painful pleasure. And it was still later that we were able to reconstruct that the patient's own genitals had been traumatically overstimulated by her mother, who had long red nails (the bloody spear!). So yes, the countertransference phenomena can be burdensome but we must not overlook their informative potential.

Results. Dr. Margolis suggests that the treatment outcome with such cases may be less satisfactory than with the usual analytic cases. Phallic-oedipal issues might not get worked through to the extent ordinarily possible. Extratransference work might be significant, and even predominate over transference-related work from time to time. Mourning over the actual past trauma may be incomplete, intermittent, even lifelong. Some patients might always carry the traumatic effects of the past incestuous experiences—"the attenuated marks of soul murder" (Shengold 1989, p. 67). Nonetheless, the ability to recall, know, and stand for truth, however terrible, itself heals the superego's contradictions, reduces the need for gross defensive operations, enhances tolerance for the chronic inner rage, and diminishes the proclivity for active or passive, sadistic or masochistic repetitions. And this is no mean achievement!

I would like to make one last point. This pertains to the manner in which the two patients in this report are identified: John Brown (referred to as "John") and *Mrs.* Martha Stone (referred to as "Mrs. Stone"). Now, the simplest explanation for addressing them differently is that Dr. Margolis first saw John when he was 19 years old and Mrs. Stone when she was 55; addressing him with his first name and her with her last name would thus seem quite reasonable. However, I wonder if there could be deeper reasons for this difference. Is it possible, for instance, that the three people in the chapter, that is, *Dr.* Margolis, *Mrs.* Stone, and John actually constitute an unconsciously nuclear family in which the generational boundaries have not been breached and the "rule of the father" (Chasseguet-Smirgel 1984) is beyond question? To subtly interpose such a healthy family within a paper dealing with incest would of course alleviate the anxiety felt in dealing with such a topic. More important, it would minimize the horror we feel at such transgressions, and mute similar desires, however remote, within ourselves.

REFERENCES

Akhtar, S. (1984). The syndrome of identity diffusion. *American Journal of Psychiatry* 141:1381–1385.

——— (1991). Panel report: sadomasochism in perversions. *Journal of the American Psychoanalytic Association.*

Blum, H. P. (1979). On the concept and consequence of the primal scene. *Psychoanalytic Quarterly* 48:27–47.

Chasseguet-Smirgel, J. (1984). *Creativity and Perversion.* New York: Norton.

Deutsch, H. (1942). Some forms of emotional disturbances and their relationship to schizophrenia. *Psychoanalytic Quarterly* 11:301–321.

Fairbairn, W. R. D. (1952). *An Object Relations Theory of Personality.* New York: Basic Books.

Frank, A. (1969). The unrememberable and the unforgettable: passive primal repression. *Psychoanalytic Study of the Child* 24:48–77. New York: International Universities Press.

Freud, S. (1914). Remembering, repeating and working through. *Standard Edition* 12:145–156.

——— (1915). Repression. *Standard Edition* 14:141–158.

——— (1916). Some character types met with in psychoanalytic work. *Standard Edition* 14:309–333.

——— (1939). Moses and monotheism. *Standard Edition* 23:73–75.

Guntrip, H. (1969). *Schizoid Phenomena, Object Relations and the Self.* New York: International Universities Press.

Jacobson, E. (1954). The "exceptions": an elaboration of Freud's character study. *Psychoanalytic Study of the Child* 14:135–154. New York: International Universities Press.

Johnson, A. M., and Szurek, S. (1952). The genesis of acting out in children and adults. *Psychoanalytic Quarterly* 21:323–352.

Kernberg, O. F. (1967). Borderline personality organization. *Journal of the American Psychoanalytic Association* 15:641.

——— (1980). *Internal World and External Reality.* New York: Jason Aronson.

Khan, M. M. R. (1971). Infantile neurosis as a false-self organization. *Psychoanalytic Quarterly* 40:425.

Kilingmo, B. (1989). Conflict and deficit: implications for technique. *International Journal of Psycho-Analysis* 70:65–79.

Kohut, H. (1971). *The Analysis of the Self*. New York: International Universities Press.

Kramer, S. (1983). Object-coercive doubting: a pathological defensive response to maternal incest. *Journal of the American Psychoanalytic Association* 31:325–351.

—— (1987). A contribution to the concept "the exception" as a developmental phenomenon. *Child Abuse and Neglect* 11:367–370.

—— (1990). Residues of incest. In *Adult Analysis and Childhood Incest*, ed. Howard Levin, pp. 149–170. Hillsdale, NJ: Analytic Press.

Litin, E., Griffin, M., and Johnson, A. M. (1956). Parental influence in unusual sexual behavior in children. *Psychoanalytic Quarterly* 25:37–55.

Mahler, M. S., Bergman, A., and Pine, F. (1975). *The Psychological Birth of the Human Infant*. New York: Basic Books.

Margolis, M. (1977). A preliminary study of a case of consummated mother–son incest. *Annual of Psychoanalysis* 5:267–293.

—— (1984). A case of mother–adolescent son incest: a follow-up study. *Psychoanalytic Quarterly* 53:355–385.

Shengold, L. (1989). *Soul Murder*. New Haven, CT: Yale University Press.

Wallerstein, R. S. (1983). Self psychology and "classical" psychoanalytic psychology: the nature of their relationship. In *The Future of Psychoanalysis*, ed. A. Goldberg, pp. 19–63. New York: International Universities Press.

Winnicott, D. W. (1960). Ego distortion in terms of true and false self. In *The Maturational Process and the Facilitating Environment*, pp. 140–152. New York: International Universities Press, 1965.

6

PSYCHICAL
TRANSFORMATIONS
BY A CHILD OF INCEST

Maurice Apprey, Ph.D.

Modern historicist accounts in the theory of knowledge in the tradition of Michel Foucault (1972) and Hayden White (1989) recognize the limits of historical representation. Recently, the historian Jacques Barzun (1968) acknowledged that he had formerly been engaged in "the strange ritual of teaching it" (p. 19). For him, teaching history had become strange, because properly, history "can only be read" (p. 19). Commenting on Barzun's theory of history, White (1989) wrote that history is "primarily *a certain kind of relation to 'the past'* mediated by a distinctive kind of written discourse" (p. 19, emphasis is mine).

Foucault (1972) discouraged historical accounts that attempt the near-impossible task of revealing stable and coherent accounts by covering history with "*a thick layer of events*" (p. 3, emphasis added). He admonished us to turn our attention away from vast entities like centuries to ruptures, gaps, discontinuities, and epistemological thresholds.

Like modern historians, child analysts are very familiar with the gaps in the history of their children that parents provide. Psychoanalytic practitioners in general observe at the diagnostic stage the admixture of historical data with psychic reality. We watch historical accounts retold, reworked, and overturned as we discover why particular historical accounts had to be told in a *particular way*. The function of the mode of telling thus gains primacy. How do analysands protect themselves from knowing? When are they ready to tell the truth to themselves or about themselves to another person? These and related questions gain pride of place in psychoanalytic inquiry. In his book *What Do You Get When You Cross a Dandelion with a Rose?* Volkan (1984) reported on a case in which his analysand gave a historical account of a younger brother that reportedly received inordinate attention, while the analysand saw himself as one who received less attention. In the third year of analysis, the analysand reported that he himself was actually the one who received excessive attention—to the point of being overstimulated and smothered. At the time he told the first story he needed to see his younger brother that way to communicate aspects of his sibling rivalry. In the second story, in which he was able to recognize himself as the recipient of the overstimulation and the smothering, he had now become aware of a piece of his history where because of a skin ailment, he had to wear a straw hat and receive a variety of body ministrations. He was now able to appropriate a piece of his own history to share his insight that a human being can be neglected as much by *too much attention* as he can be by *lack of attention*.

In any historical account of incest we must pay attention to transformations of facts into personal fictions, as it were. What renders these psychical transformations stable? Paul Pruyser (1983) asked: "What needs to happen for the first faint images to become articulate, stable, available to recall, and to form as it were a collection whose items can be conjured up when needed and whose parts or qualities can be separated, recombined in all kinds of patterns, and *tinkered with*?" (pp. 23–24). For Pruyser (1983), following Winnicott (1951), the answer lies in the play of the imagination "if not the imagination itself, which has produced the arts, the sciences, religion, and several of the culture's lesser goods as well" (p. 24). Also, for Pruyser the answer lies in Margaret Mahler's (1975) separation–individuation phase. Specifically, we arrange stable mental imagery on our developmental journey as we engage ourselves in the task of "the practicing of the imagination" (p. 24) as a way station *toward* self and object constancy.

In thinking about incest in clinical stories we must not only observe the arrangement of stable mental imagery to mediate ruptures, discontinuities, and gaps as a technique in providing an illusion of self-continuity, we must also observe how psychical arrangements and rearrangements become part of the ego's task; a rearrangement that Heinz Hartmann (1958) called "change of function" (p. 25). When there is a change of function "a behavior-form which originated in a certain realm of life may, in the course of development, appear in an entirely different realm and role. An attitude which arose in the service of defense against an instinctual drive may, in the course of time, become an independent structure . . . (pp. 25–26). Thus, what was once a goal toward finding a means of self-protection could become a goal in its own right at a later stage in development. Elsewhere in a related passage, Hartmann (1958) wrote:

> What was originally anchored in instincts may subsequently be performed in the service of and by means of the ego, though, naturally, new regulations too will arise in the course of development of the ego and the id. Differentiation progresses not only by the creation of new apparatuses to master new demands and new tasks, but also and mainly by new apparatuses taking over, on a higher level, functions which were originally performed by more primitive means. [pp. 49–50]

We are therefore discouraged from looking for linear causal relations between childhood and later stages of development. This would be a genetic fallacy. Thus, separation–individuation tasks in childhood are quite distinct from those in adulthood, although aspects of the former will be infused in the latter.

If there are ruptures in clinical and historical stories, if the play of the imagination mediates these ruptures by arranging or rearranging stable mental imagery to fill in the narrative, if, furthermore, a change of function occurs in how one psychically transforms a childhood mode of mediation into an adult mode of mediation, what system of protection does the incest victim employ to organize her world?

To answer this question I suggest we move from novelty of content to form in the way we engage our patients in the history-taking process and beyond. For example, what secrets there are must ultimately give the pride of place to modes of *mystification* of these secrets, whatever they are and wherever they lie.

Within the horizon of this notion of mystification are the theory of "deferred action" (Freud 1900), the idea of "secret as potential space" (Khan 1983), and the idea of "personal myth" (Kris 1956). All these ideas point to a mode of revision that André Green (1973) articulated so clearly: "One major capacity of the psychic structure is the capacity *to cut off, to suspend an experience, while it is still going on*. This is not for the purpose of the observing the experience as in the conscious mental functioning, but to shut off the awareness of it in order to *recreate* it, in one's way later on" (Khan 1983, p. 100, emphasis added).

Other ideas that are continuous with the thought of suspending, deferring, or circumscribing an event in order to give it a personal and transformed meaning are Freud's (1900) notions of condensation, displacement, symbolization, secondary revision, and identity of perception. All these processes guide André Green's (1973) admonition that: "It is important to see that this cutting off or inner splitting is a precondition for the establishment of further links by association. We should distinguish the moment of the experience and the moment in which it becomes meaningful" (Khan 1983, p. 100).

By emphasizing mystification, I wish to acknowledge Freud (1900), Kris (1956), Green (1973), and Khan (1983), and what is more important, extend our inquiry into specific activities that occur when we freeze a historical experience long enough to find a consonant contemporary experience that would facilitate the transformation of that experience. Mystification as a concept collapses the precedent-setting ideas of Freud, Kris, Green, and Khan to look at the specific way in which the objective is subjectivized and presented as bifurcated but continuous: inside and outside, present and absent, part and whole, high and deep. In other words, we mask one image with another that is apparently different, only to find upon close scrutiny that the two behaviors are the same description of an anterior experience, only rewritten within a new and yet associatively linked context.

To come to grips with these modes of mystification that protect patients from knowing or from seeing more clearly or from seeing what place secrecy-laden events have in their lives, we need a new mode of response to how clinical stories are presented to us. In other words, when our patients tell us stories of their lives, with all their ruptures, gaps, and discontinuities, we too must have tools for grasping how they (patients) fill in these epistemic gaps.

I will outline one such tool, which I call a system of mutual implications, for it relies on unpacking ambivalence, ironies, conflicts, and the like. It assumes that modes of mystification and other techniques that patients use to fill in the ruptures in their clinical stories utilize multiple ambivalent, ambitendent, conflicting, and Janusian strategies that confound their recall and retelling. Behind this assumption as to how patients fill in their narratives lies a notion of incest attack that says that when a person's physical space is invaded, a hollow mental space is created. The victim goes in search of her ideal self; an ideal, untainted self that in reality will never be found. She will therefore fill in this new space with illusions that can at best be stepping-stones, bridge-building figurative tropes, fictive theories, and metaphors that only promise to provide a sense of self-continuity. Behind the thick layer of historical events, a particular kind of relation to the past will be remembered in action, acted out; reenacted with a new set of dramatis personae. This very act of retelling, recalling, and recasting is a paradoxical instrument; on the one hand, an event has been displaced and altered in the process, and yet on the other hand this same event, which reveals a particular mode of relating to the past, shows itself as a present mode of integration and of relating to one's contemporary world. In other words, it is no longer a passive experience of history, but rather an active element of determining one's present and future relations. It was once an isolated unit of historical experience. Now, it constitutes a general history.

To schematize the system of mutual implications, I have drawn on the consistent features of descriptions on incest and seduction in general described by Maurice Merleau-Ponty (1964), Margaret Mead (1950), Sandor Ferenczi (1933), and Jean Laplanche (1989). Out of these descriptions, I have isolated those features that resonate with my clinical and research experience. I have isolated those features that point to ambitendencies, ambivalences, ironies, and conflicts to show that a system of mutualities, complicities, and reciprocities lurk behind the fact of incest occurrence and the theorizing about it. What are some of these ambitendencies or figurative tropes that juxtapose two mutually implicated aspects of human nature?

AMBITENDENT TROPES BEHIND
A SYSTEM OF MUTUAL IMPLICATIONS
IN THE STORY OF INCEST

Ambitendent tropes or figurations that present themselves in psychoanalytic inquiry of incest include, as Merleau-Ponty (1964, p. 120) puts it, "The universal fact is that children exist, that they start out small and weak, but are closely associated with adult life. We therefore find a 'premature double blooming of sexual feeling in the child unready for procreation' (Mead 1950, p. 127). The child's experience is polarized around sexual questions, but it is at the same time incapable of performing the characteristic activities of an adult." In this ambitendent trope, the smallness of the child is juxtaposed to his or her interests in the sexuality of adults.

In a second ambitendent trope, the physical strength of the adult incest perpetrator is juxtaposed to his or her emotional weakness or emotional immaturity.

Laplanche (1987–1989) is correct when he equates the adult's action in incest to a bungled action that reveals not only adult irresponsibility and immaturity but also an unconscious primal and deep-seated desire in human nature. Let Laplanche speak to the mutuality of the adult as adult and the child housed in the adult:

> Given that the child lives on in the adult, an adult faced with a child is particularly likely to be deviant and inclined to perform bungled or even symbolic actions because *he is involved in a relationship with his other self*, with *the other he once was. The child in front of him brings out the child within him.* The primal relationship is therefore established on a twofold register: We have both a vital, open and reciprocal relationship, which can truly be said to be interactive, and a relationship which is implicitly sexual, where there is no interaction because *the two partners are not partners.* [p. 103, emphasis is mine]

There is a semblance of relationship at the vital and primal level when a syncretic and asymbolic mode of relatedness operates. However, there is no relationship at the human order. There is, rather, a bungled adult action in which both concrete and unconscious ideation are implicated.

In the third ambitendent trope, the fact of incest occurrence is juxtaposed with theory. In other words, the actuality of incest alternates with theories driven by the play of imagination. When the fact disappears, its psychic transformatioñ occurs. When the theory or psychic transformation disappears, the fact occurs. Or, as Laplanche (1978–1989) puts it "they appear and disappear together" (p. 104). It is this alteration of appearance and disappearance of fact and theory that belies and drives mystification and the heuristic problems it poses in psychoanalytic inquiry of incest.

The fourth ambitendent trope is continuous with the third. The theory of incest now is bifurcated into a two-stage theory that, according to Laplanche (1978–1989), "shows that it is only because it becomes *auto-traumatic* that a trauma has a pathogenic effect" (p. 112). In other words, the immanent aspects of the trauma or the trauma-as-remembered through a second and new scene is that which is implicated in the pathological formation.

In short, it is suggested here that gaps and ruptures in continuity of one's self can be filled in by personal theories of historical contexts as remembered in the form of personal theories. In the clinical story to follow an adolescent has a personal theory, informed by psychic reality, to fill in the gaps in her sense of self-continuity. That personal theory revolves around the invariant fantasy that light-skinned blacks must not be trusted, because "they are sneaky." The ambitendent trope here is light skin/dark skin, light black/dark black.

CASE ILLUSTRATION

I present one of the cases that drew my attention to a mode of mystification of family sexual secrets, incest, and the ambitendencies that lie behind mystification and other confounding facets that impede psychoanalytic discovery. The part of the work given here is largely the extended diagnostic portion. Let me emphasize that this is not a psychoanalysis of an adolescent. Rather, psychoanalytic observation is used to come to grips with conscious and unconscious matter as they show themselves in an interdisciplinary service-oriented research program that allowed the infusion of psychoanalytic understanding into a variety of treatment modalities.

The Setting: Adolescent Pregnancy Project

The clinical material that forms the basis of this presentation comes from the therapeutic contact with one of my caseloads in an adolescent pregnancy program. This project was an integral part of the N.I.M.H. (National Institute of Mental Health)-sponsored clinical infant development program, a clinical research and service program. A primary purpose of the adolescent pregnancy program was to learn more about adolescence, how pregnancy enhances or presents impediments to psychological development, and how babies develop with their adolescent mothers. The program offered prenatal and postnatal services to all subject-participants for eighteen to twenty-four months of the baby's life. Intervention was made through individual and group psychotherapies, counseling, psychological, and developmental assessments, preparation for childbirth and parenthood, developmental guidance for mothers, and liaison/consultation services involving school, medical, and social agencies. This was very much a multidisciplinary program, and it was the task of a primary clinician to help the research participant consolidate gains made through contact with all members of the team. The material presented focuses primarily on how my work with the adolescent participant on her major preoccupation, that is, the search for her biological father, fits into an overall context in her development. We shall learn in the process a great deal about the inner world of an adolescent in search of her biological father when she knows and does not know that she is the product of incest. We shall also learn how this ineffable situation is couched in her statement: *I hate light-skinned blacks; they are sneaky.*

Early Reflections on the Meaning of Pregnancy
for the Adolescent

The meaning of pregnancy in the total context of a person's development is no doubt multifaceted. To become pregnant and to have the baby may ostensibly fulfill fantasies of motherhood—motherhood as a developmental stage wherein one becomes like one's mother, and thus actualizes the yearnings of an earlier developmental period. Psychoanalytic observations, however, gives us access to a wider repertoire of such internal issues as concerns about one's body integrity, the fantasied cancerous content of one's body, such important feelings as disappointment or even disillusionment for carrying or giving birth to a damaged child, as well as ambivalence or destructive urges toward the product of one's own body. These important feelings may be irrational, but real enough to have an impact on one's view of self as caregiver or on the mother's investment in the child.

In the same way, it does not seem to be a comprehensive enough observation to stop at observing pregnancy in adolescence as a severance step away from the mother. Pregnancies in adolescence have multiple meanings, and each one provides a rich profile as to how humans function. For my clinical practice, I observe that a pregnancy may conceivably be the adolescent girl's use of a boyfriend to express hatred toward her mother as a way of freeing herself from the internal image of the mother in the attempt to gain the desired measure of autonomy. In cases where there is a hatred of the mother, the young adolescent mother may indeed succeed in producing a replica of herself through her own child, who may be narcissistically cathected. Nevertheless, this hatred undermines the pleasure expected of the childbearing process. The result is almost invariably an ambivalent cathexis of the child that compromises the development of both the child and its adolescent mother.

The struggle between the pregnant adolescent girl and her mother is an intriguing one that merits close study. Each individual case has its own fascination. The adolescent girl described here, when asked why she was quick to dismiss breast feeding, answered, "It isn't me." In a manifest sense it is not like her to breast feed her baby. In a latent sense she offers us a handle for understanding the feeling of being an imposter in her pregnancy: "I am not really a mother." Her conscious feelings of competence are threatened by her unconscious aggressive impulses: impulses that have failed to undergo repression, impulses against the "bad" mother that can result in depression, fear that the baby would scoop out the content of her breasts, thanks to his greed and that she would pass the "gas" in her own food, like "pizza," onto the child. Owning her feelings even further during this same period, her own inner feeling of ugliness that was very observable in the neonatal period betrayed her hidden fear of destroying the relationship with her child. What is "bad," or rather frustrating, about the mother of this adolescent girl is that she hid the identity of the girl's father from her, hence his anonymity. All that is known of him is that father *is a light-skinned black man.* The only light-skinned child among her siblings, this adolescent's complexion is a painful reminder to her that she is different from the other children in the family. Thus, her hatred of her father as the "light black" who is "sneaky" or, more specifically, "sneaked out" on her; likewise, her hatred of her mother for hiding his identity, and who is thereby experienced as his accomplice. An interesting derivative of the unconscious aggressive impulses toward her mother is that when this girl is angry with her mother she hides her purse or some other valuable item that her mother would be likely to look for.

How do I use the black/white cultural stereotypes that often express indirectly the personal symptomatology and conflicts of my patients, black and white alike, in Euro-American cultural contexts in which the constellation of blackness/lightness/whiteness is a criterion for interpersonal comparison and self-image? To answer this question, I will preface my response with the information that I am a Ghanaian, an African, who grew up in Ghana and has spent a third of my life in Britain and the United States. Having spent practically all of my adult life away from home, I write about my observations of the Euro-American world with the embroidery of my own African cultural heritage. Having grown up in Ghana where the black indigenous people have always been a majority, I have had to renegotiate my own notion of blackness in this "new" world where the black race is a minority group, and where skin color is consciously or unconsciously a factor in the way black and white alike define their personal and social needs and negotiate their self-concept. In the course of my analytic and psychotherapeutic work, both black and white patients cathect me with a repertoire of feelings that include fear, admiration, envy, hatred. Upon me they let loose their externalizations and projections, and in the course of the analysis or psychotherapy they find themselves dealing with unacceptable impulses in themselves, primal scene fantasies, beating fantasies, and an intriguing range of concerns lurking behind their cathexis of treatment. The adolescent described here saw me as "brilliant" and used our alliance to puzzle out her confusions. While she idealized me, I felt as if I were on a journey or treasure hunt with her. Seeing me in my blackness, she seized upon some noticeable differences between us to define her evolving sense of self.

Description, Family Background, and Personal History

Fay is a 16-year-old girl who is pleasant, gregarious, and talkative. She is very likeable, dresses quite well, and engages others with her ever-present sense of curiosity.

Ms. T., aged 35, the girl's mother, came to see me at my request. I wanted to get some background information, most of all to get an impression of Fay's maternal environment. Ms. T. wanted to be helpful and indeed was.

Thinking that Fay's early experiences were uneventful, she tried to give me a rather hilarious account of how Fay as a little girl used to "tell tales to her teacher and to the neighbors." These tales had to do with Fay's fantasy that she had to change schools. These tales aroused people's curiosity and gave them something to laugh about when they discovered that there was no external reality to her stories. When she was 5, she and her younger brother would on occasion go out for a walk, until some neighbor recognized them and took them back home. Fay, of course, knew she "only" lived "up the road." The only story inconsistent with her moving tales is one in which she told of an accident on the road with ambulances coming up to the scene, and so forth, only for her mother to discover it was untrue.

Fay at around the age of 4 reportedly showed a distinct dislike for playing with dolls when dolls were first introduced to her by her mother. She would rather play with puzzles, pencils, and paper, and the like. Her mother was intrigued but had no thoughts about what it meant.

Fay had her menarche at age 11, according to her mother. Fay hated it and constantly asked why it had happened to her, that is, why she had to menstruate. She has hated it until now. Tired of carrying the baby around for nearly nine months, she thought she would rather be menstruating than being heavy with child.

She has no girlfriends, according to her mother, and tends to be more at ease with male acquaintances than with females. Nevertheless, she has been a pleasant, likeable, gregarious person all her life. She settled well in school. Indeed, from her mother I get the feeling that Fay has no real concerns or difficult areas in her life. According to her mother, not even the absence of Fay's father seemed at this point worrying to her, empathic though she herself appears to be as a mother. Fay was special to her mother, and it is this very specialness that mitigated the extent of her hurt when she learned of her daughter's pregnancy. Fay's mother had not anticipated in any way that this might happen.

The mother herself spoke of her own mother's death when she was 8 years of age. She lived on a small farm near Vienna, Virginia, then. She was left with a father who seemed relieved by the death of his controlling wife and reveled in his newfound freedom. Subsequent to her death, he neglected his daughter. Ms. T. was the youngest of three daughters. The two older siblings had both left home. The father had a girlfriend he never married, but whose children he fathered materially and emotionally as though they were his own. He gave these children money and whatever they needed. This was done in front of Ms. T. to the point where the children's mother wondered aloud why the father gave his daughter nothing but gave things to the other children in front of his daughter, upsetting as it was for her. Ms. T. said she never let her father know that it hurt so much; instead, she cried in private. This situation went on until she was 14.

At 15 she gave birth to her first child, a son who was raised by Ms. T.'s sister, Sarah, who is older by some twenty years. This older sister had lost her first and only son only hours after delivery. She had a series of miscarriages, and greatly involved herself in the rearing of Ms. T.'s children. Fay was the third child and reportedly an offspring of a different father from that of the others, who reportedly share one father. Fay's mother's involvement in the rearing of her own children has heretofore been minimal. This lack of involvement prompted one child neighbor to ask Fay if her family had a maid in the house—that fantasied maid being Fay's real mother. Ms. T. denied being upset by this reference to her as a maid and insisted that she felt like a real mother of her children. The children themselves thought of the aunt as their mother, and of their real mother as a young aunt. Thus the roles between the two sisters were reversed.

Ms. T. spoke about her irritation at Fay's almost obsessional traits, for instance, her need to carry an extra set of earrings, extra clothes, and personal belongings even when she was away for an overnight visit. She spoke about Fay's not being very domesticated and wondered whether Fay had enough regard for her boyfriend, who is the father of the child she is carrying.

Ms. T. spoke of the numerous quarrels between Fay and her boyfriend, wondering why they argued but having no desire to interfere.

Finally, I wondered about her hesitation to talk with Fay about her father. She explained that she had not seen him for a period of about ten years, and that since each time she did see him he was in the company of his wife, she thought it improper to discuss Fay with him. Consequently, she did not know if the father thought about Fay. Also, she would like to think of her contact with Fay's father as a thing of the past, the reawakening of which seemed superfluous to her. Nevertheless, I saw the secrecy surrounding the identity of the father as willful withholding.

There was nothing eventful about Fay's early feeding experiences except that she never liked eggs. She walked at age 1, was toilet trained easily at 1½, had no hesitation settling in school, and remained an active, curious child.

At the time of her daughter's adolescent pregnancy Ms. T. was 35, yet looked considerably older. I thought she was in her late forties or even early fifties when I first met her. She worked as a cleaning woman, a domestic for seven families, some of whom were public figures. She stated with humor that the job was quite easy and that any difficulty she had at work had more to do with remembering who she was working for on any one occasion than with the actual amount of work. She wanted to go back to school to learn to be a helper with elderly people or to work as some kind of aide in a helping agency. In retrospect I see that with or without school she was still bent on cleaning up.

Possible Significant Environmental Influences

Secrecy surrounding father's absence. Fay did not know her father and longed to know who he was, where he is, all about him. She longed to tell him how angry she was with him and to ask why he did not "come looking for me." "If I see him I would wring his neck. . . . He'd have to pay for all that time somebody else looked after me," Fay insisted. Her mother acknowledged that she had hitherto underestimated the importance of talking to Fay about her father and that she may have erred in this respect. Fay still tried to work out oedipal issues, and her father's anonymity, enforced by her mother's secretiveness, had not helped in this regard.

Mother's delegation of caretaking functions to her own sister, who was twenty years older, with the result that Ms. T. was cathected as a sibling by her own children. There was, thus, a question as to the quality of intimacy and relatedness between the mother and Fay. Ms. T.'s "sibling" relationship with her children did serve as a defense against the precarious certainty of herself as mother.

The mother's diminished sense of self, which was evident in a neighbor's child wondering if she was a maid instead of the mother. The neglect and cruel treatment of the mother by the father and her own mother's death could only accentuate the hurt and poor self-image of Fay's mother. Fay's awareness of her mother's own plight somewhat softened her rage toward her. In Fay's fantasy, however, it could be her mother's fault that Fay's father left.

Her mother's pregnancies, from age 15, which she told Fay were in response to losing her own mother at age 8.

Feeling that she was missing out on the attention lavished on her older sister, a teenage parent like herself, Fay may conceivably have sought to be like her sister; a position perceived by her as enviable. Fay originally said she wanted a girl, but seeing that her sister had a girl, she changed her mind and said she wanted a boy, which she now has.

DESCRIPTIVE DIAGNOSTIC SUMMARY

Although Fay exhibits the outward trappings of age-adequate adolescent development and demonstrates many areas of intact ego-functioning (for example, academically, and with her apparent social skills and competencies), there appear to be deep-seated ego deficits, markedly in the area of reality testing.

She has progressed from a constricted latency, in which there was limited engagement, to same-sex peers without her earlier unresolved conflicts presenting major hurdles. The pregnancy and childbearing process have accentuated these developmental obstacles.

There is a basic structural problem and a deficit in reality testing that her defense organization at present appears inadequate to deal with. The threat of regression into disorganization does exist for her when stress is too great. She seems to fear disorganization due to her aggressive and sadistic wishes. To defend against this fear of fragmentation, she has devised compulsive measures, such as carrying with her extra earrings and an extra set of clothes, to give her a sense of body intactness and self-sufficiency. She uses these defenses to assure herself and her environment that she and her environment are intact and organized. She externalizes onto others the basis for her disorganization. Although there is a deficit in reality testing and the threat of her aggressive impulses still exists, this has not reached a paranoid level. The pregnancy did make the threat of regression more predominant and more anxiety producing. This threat of regression was inseparable from her fantasy of feeling empty and deflated or of evaporating as she anticipated delivery and its aftermath.

In the prenatal period there seemed to be a wide swing in the range of her ego development, exaggerated though the picture was by the pregnancy. Postnatally, there has been relative ego strength in her functioning. Postnatally, there is still evidence of fixation in oral, anal–sadistic, and oedipal phases. In terms of personality organization, her ego boundaries have a relative firmness but become relatively fluid under stress. There is still a great concern with aggressive and sadistic wishes at unconscious and preconscious levels, and she strives for control and containment. Fay's concerns about sneakiness in black men with light complexions is gradually pointing the way to family secrets that she explores in relationship to herself and to the anonymity of her father. In search of her father, she seems to fear punishment for her own secret, aggressive, retaliatory wishes. While her excessive talk of food points to oral fixation, her obsessional traits point to anal fixation, and the vigorous effort to discover/rediscover her father to fixation at the oedipal phase. Some of Fay's concerns about body damage, in which she linked the anticipated pain of labor to breaking both her arms, point to early gender-identity conflicts that resurfaced with the issue of pregnancy.

Fay reveals an ambivalent reaction to dependency. In the "doll interview" in which I instructed her to hold a doll and imagine what her reactions to her own baby would be like, there was a strong negative reaction that had a curious admixture of anxiety and manic relief. She refused to hold it and apologized for the refusal. She insisted, "Give me a Barbie doll, and I will hold it any day." At the age of 4 she showed a distinct aversion for baby dolls and a liking for the more adult-looking, sensual Barbie dolls. In the course of her development, she made a leap from helplessness and a mistrust in her objects of dependency to a semblance of higher developmental levels. Because she had learned to be distrustful of dependency, she uses the fantasy of the image of her anonymous father to work out dependence needs and issues, as well as oedipal ones. Turning passive into active, she deals with separation anxiety by being the one who leaves, and thus makes use of fantasy to deal with painful reality. Fay's mother has given her the message that one replaces loss by getting pregnant, and in this pregnancy, Fay, through identification, has followed her mother's example and may well have actualized her mother's fantasies. Recall that Fay's mother had lost her mother. Fay's mother has herself said that she was looking for a father—a better one than her own father, who mistreated her—and replacing her mother by being herself a mother of three children.

Fay's pregnancy seems to have been an attempt at resolution of body-damage concerns, including the issues of damage and missing body parts. The pregnancy was therefore aimed at adaptation, but in the process aroused conflicts at being damaged by the delivery and by the baby. The pregnancy was also an attempt to identify with female figures, and thus resolve internal conflicts over femininity versus masculinity to prove to herself her body adequacy and ultimately to organize around the childbearing process the link between representations of femininity with the mature female genital, with a view to negotiating the final sexual organization in adolescence.

THERAPEUTIC STRATEGY

To help her in her development as a caretaker, effort must be made to help her map out demarcation lines between her own developmental issues and her baby's, so that she does not misinterpret cues from her baby or attribute her own concerns (such as her own helplessness) to the baby. Individual and group work would help her gain a greater sense of self and to foster some degree of closeness to peers. Work must be done to help her tolerate her baby's dependency needs without seeing him as a rival.

The evidence so far is that despite the initial shock of having to cope as a caretaker for an easily distressed child, she has learned some methods of her own to calm her baby. Music, which at the outset was unsettling for this baby, is now used by Fay to soothe him.

The greatest task, however, is helping her make the shift from her cathexis of father as structure, a visibly present concrete fact, to father as a symbol and process without taking anything away from the genuine need to see her father in person. Father as symbol and process shifts the emphasis from the concrete biological fact to the essence of psychological fathering that lends itself to internalization of an adult's ego and superego attributes. In this regard, Fay saw her uncle as one who has done an adequate job as her psychological father.

Having looked at Fay from the broader developmental diagnostic picture, we could duly return to the vicissitudes of her search for her father in the overall context of oedipal concerns. However, first a word about the preoedipal period. We know from Fay's disgust with age-appropriate baby dolls that she could not bear to play with these because they were "helpless" and dependent; that in spite of substitute mothering from her mother's sister, Fay still mistrusts her objects of dependency; that there is oral fixation. We know from her precocious attachment to the more sexually mature Barbie dolls that she was unprepared to negotiate the oedipal phase, thanks to the relative lack of preparation from the preoedipal phase. Having barely tinkered with the oedipal phase, she very precariously moved on into latency.

With the epigenetic push toward puberty, oedipal and preoedipal issues were rekindled and the quality of her school-work began to deteriorate. She detested her menstrual period and still continued with her tentative but progressive developmental steps. The attachment to her boyfriend seems to have been her second chance to work through the dissolution of the oedipal concerns. Here the opportunity exists for her to become more successful at holding on to her boyfriend. Having had a male child with this boyfriend has also contributed to a further opportunity to see the reemergence of the Oedipus complex after its prior dissolution in the context of the relationship with the boyfriend, the baby's father.

The resolution of Fay's developmental issues in the early stages of treatment were confounded by her mother's own developmental struggles. In my work with Ms. T., whom I saw at intervals of approximately once a month, she cooperated to the extent that she could allow herself. Feeling pressured by Fay to assist her in finding her father, Ms. T. matched Fay's determined resolve with an equally resolute posture that her daughter should not see her father. At the outset she seemed to be protecting Fay from being hurt just in case her father did not want her. Further exploration revealed that the mother feared her own longing for Fay's father. This yearning for him became patently clear to her when she reportedly met the father in a supermarket with his wife. Even though she and Fay's father pretended they did not see each other, she was sure he saw her and might have spoken if he had not been with his wife. She admitted that it pained her that he was inaccessible to her. By the third interview, Fay's mother was aware of her own needs getting in her daughter's way, but she remained resolute nevertheless. Her own unresolved developmental struggles kept pulling her back. She recalled how cruelly her own father had treated her; how her closeness with her mother was interrupted by her death; how she sought a man to take care of her by getting pregnant at age 14 or 15.

She was relieved to be able to cry and share these important thoughts with me. This was the first time she had talked with anyone about her sadness at her mother's death; her anger at father for rejecting her; her guilt that she was not home when her own mother died. Her oedipal issues soon gave way to preoedipal concerns, although initially she talked about her own dependency needs by displacing them. She spoke of how insatiate her two daughters were, how one of them left home in search of gratification from her boyfriend's mother, and how Fay was finding it difficult to leave home and prepare to get married. When it dawned on me that she was working about twenty miles from where she lived and going to great lengths to work as a cleaner in Vienna, Virginia, I wondered if she could do the same job closer to her home. She said: "I guess I am still looking for something back there." Vienna is where she grew up. Vienna is where she had Fay. There she longed to repair her traumatic childhood, with all the disappointment in her parents and in Fay's father.

As a result of my individual work with Fay, she came to intimate that it was more crucial to understand the impact of her father's anonymity on her overall development than actually to see father, that is, his symbolic, internal meaning was beginning to override the present possibility of his being a concrete father. Also, since her longing to see father was causing her mother so much pain, she wondered whether she should continue to alienate her mother. The mother was now an important person in helping her deal with her difficulties in getting married and leaving home. There were clearly enormous oedipal and pre-oedipal issues that had to be worked on, and, aware of them, Fay had the determination to follow through with treatment. She felt that treatment should come first, and if she should renew her striving to see her father, she would postpone the search until she was old enough to find him without her mother's permission.

Fay's search for her father can be discussed under the headings that Ricoeur (1974) suggests: "(1) the formation of the Oedipus complex, (2) the destruction of the Oedipus complex, and (3) the permanence of the Oedipus complex" (pp. 468–497). Under the rubric of the formation of the Oedipus complex, we can see how Fay's desire for her father showed in the anger toward her mother for hiding his identity and the ambivalent cathexis of the father as an object she longed to make contact with and a target of her aggression for deserting her. Under the rubric of the passing of the Oedipus complex, we can see how important Fay's boyfriend was to her—someone who would marry her and give her an independent life, except that her separation anxiety still undermined her efforts to separate from her infantile objects. Last, the permanence of the Oedipus complex shows in the strong wish to give birth to a boy—a boy who would be a cross between her light skin, which she thinks came from her father, and the dark complexion of her boyfriend (a symbolic compromise). The job of having to raise this boy instead of a girl, the wish to see whether there was a resemblance between her son and her anonymous father, inter alia, were pointers to the shift from father as structure and the resurgence of father as process and symbol.

I hoped that at the end of treatment, light blacks would not remain a symbolic container of hostile feelings, a symbol of desertion, deception, mental anguish, and the like, but become whole persons in their own right. I hoped that in the course of treatment this shift would be accompanied by an effort on her part to be a person more capable of holding on to her boyfriend or husband, and that such effort would facilitate her boyfriend's fathering skills to the benefit of their son.

One appealing thing about Fay is that her material encourages me to use culture to sensitize myself to the fertile areas in clinical matter. Howard Stein (1981), in a personal communication regarding technique and cultural understanding, had this to say: "I am coming more and more to the conclusion that each new generation not only invests in culture but reinvents culture, as it comes to be represented in defenses against early object relations. One of the crucial clinical issues is, to use the words of George Devereux, how to use the patient's material as self-abolishing cultural levers, so to speak, or as crutches which first are used to walk—after which time such seemingly reified transitional objects are no longer necessary."

I liked these comments very much, and at once I am reminded that Fay, born in the early sixties, had very little direct experience of the civil rights movement, and probably does not know that it was considered an advantage to be light skinned before the civil rights movement restored pride to those black in complexion. In Fay's personal myth, thanks to her developmental issues, light black has come to be distinct disadvantage. One can already see the strength of Stein's observation that each new generation not only cathects culture but reinvents it in a way that encompasses one's own defenses and developmental vicissitudes.

Preparing for the day when Fay would learn from her mother who her father was, I focused with Fay on understanding what the essential attributes of a father were and wondered aloud who had hitherto provided fathering and made parental impressions on her. She saw the uncle in whose house they lived as the one such person, but that was not enough. A father would have to be blood father as well as psychological father. If her uncle turned out to be the blood father, she would be disgusted, feel betrayed, probably run out of the house, and prematurely leave home to get married. If, on the other hand, she had not met the father before, she would want him to make up for all the lost time by buying her material things like a car. If he did not want to bother with her, she would simply want to see him once and he could go his way. In these preparatory sessions for the discovery or rediscovery of her father, it meant a lot to Fay that her father "should not be the kind of man who simply sat at home and depended on his [working] wife." Her father, she thought, should be very much a man, a productive person.

TOWARD THE DISCOVERY OF FATHER

In a later interview with Ms. T. in which we continued to discuss Fay's wish to see her father, I asked Ms. T. if there were any items of information that I needed to know before we talked together with Fay, just in case such information came out in Fay's presence when she (Ms. T.) was unprepared to deal with it. She said, "Yes, a whole lot." "Like what?" I wondered. Ms. T.: "Like how it all happened." The longer we talked the harder it became for her to talk. The reason for this was that it would be hard for her to forgive herself, hard for her (dead) mother to forgive her if it came out of her mouth, hard for God to forgive her. Everyone would know how terrible she was for doing what she had done in bringing forth Fay the way she did. After sitting in silence with her, watching her in tears, and I surmised that whatever it was we could work with it constructively, and as such, it was better out, dealt with, and given a decent burial than hidden, only to cause her more and more guilt and remorse. She decided that she would as a first step write to me. It would be easier for her that way. I agreed to how she wished to proceed with the self-disclosure and the work we had to do following the revelation of her "secret."

This is the letter I received a few days later.

June 3rd, 1981

Dear Maurice,

It is very hard for me to talk to someone in person about what I am going to write. You are the only one I ever felt like talking to about this. I love my daughter very much. Fay's father is not the person that I told you about and the one she thinks of as her father. There is such a person, but we never became that close. We even went to school together, but that's it. I guess it happened one day when I was home alone. Fay's father is my brother-in-law. It wasn't a case of rape or anything like that, it just happened, that's why it is so hard to talk about it. I have never told anyone. I am not saying which one of my brothers-in-law because I have three. Maybe I was looking for a father image or just someone to care. My sister loved me, but I was like an orphan, someone that they had to take care of, that is how they made me feel. When I got older, I didn't care about how they made me feel. I still wasn't close to my father because I guess I will always hold it against him for not taking me after my mother died. If my sisters or brothers ever found out about my life, they would think of me as an outsider. It is easy when I am at work because I can leave all my trouble behind. I guess if Fay didn't have Jake (her baby) I would always put it off about who her father is. She has been asking more and more questions for the last three years. Each year it gets harder to answer her overactive mind. She says if she ever meets her father she is going to ask him to buy her a car and help her finish school. I don't know if this is possible at this point. You will never know how many times I wished I didn't know what sex is about. I can't say love because I never had anyone love me very much. I always thought of telling Fay when she became 18, or even writing her a letter. Maybe I should have had help with this a long time ago and not let it go on. You know, if I had stayed one minute longer in your office, I think I would have broken down and told you yesterday. Sometimes I think of my life as a soap opera. I guess I should leave something for Fay to know who her father is if anything should ever happen to me in the near future.

Well, I have to close now.

Cindy

I had a session with Ms. T. a few days later. She looked at relative peace with herself. There were a few tears but not a whole lot like the week before or on previous occasions. I did not ask her which of the "uncles" Fay's father was, assuming for now that it was the husband of Fay's aunt who raised her and in whose house Fay and her mother lived together with Ms. T.'s two sons.

She explained to me how very difficult it was for her to think about writing down the information, but how much easier it was once she had begun to write. "It was a relief." She also said that Fay's father knew he was the father, but they had not talked about it for years. "He left it all up to me." I empathized: "It must be quite a burden, perhaps an unfair one, too, to be left carrying such a load and having to determine on your own whether and how Fay should be told." She smiled and said, "Yes." Further, Ms. T.'s sister did not know about this. Ms. T. thought, "She might not know, but then she might." I was impressed by how much calmer Ms. T. was that day, knowing very well that we had a lot of work to do yet and a lot of pain in the sessions ahead.

Finally, I arranged to meet with both Fay and her mother. The first joint appointment had to be canceled because Fay got "walking pneumonia." In a subsequent individual session with Fay, she said, "I guess I was afraid to find out who my father was." The next appointment at which Fay was to find out who father was, she had "a great big row" with her boyfriend and was too upset to attend the joint session. She understood in the next individual sessions that she had "nerves" about the joint session. When we finally met, her mother told her that her father was her uncle, the man who had socially fathered her all along. "It's just that you did not know it." Fay responded in horror. With tears running down her face she asked her mother: "Why didn't you tell me before? I would have understood. . . . People have been asking me for a long time. Even my counselor asked if I knew my father. . . . You know what? Lisa [a distant cousin] told me eight years ago, but I did not want to believe it. My sister thought that was just Lisa running her mouth off like she always did. . . . My sister did not want to know anyway, but I always wanted to know."

Fay and her mother decided to keep it a secret for the present. This secret seemed to unify them for now. I decided to have another joint session very soon, one in which we would decide the next move in relation to the impact of this discovery on the whole family and in what directions, as well as how, we would want to proceed. My individual work with Fay would no doubt now have to look into the shift and psychological impact on her from the perception of herself as having been reared by one biological parent to knowing she had been reared by two biological parents all along.

Dynamically, there are the questions raised by the discovery: What will happen to the old myths and defenses that once sustained her? What new defenses might she now erect? How would she negotiate ways of dealing with her separation anxiety, mistrust of dependence, and so forth–issues that were fed by the anonymity of her father? What will be the status of her cathexis of such objects as her mother, her uncle/father, her son, her boyfriend? These and other questions will be addressed another time.

So the myth that father was an elusive light black became shattered. She now accepted her mother's word that it was her grandmother who was light skinned. The personal myth couched in cultural terms was that light blacks were sneaky, and came into mother's life and left. This myth may now shift to accommodate the reality, albeit a harsh one, that the man she knew as her uncle was indeed her biological father. The man she knows as her psychological father is indeed her uncle. Furthermore, the man she now knows as her father fathered her three siblings too.

CONCLUSION

In this presentation, I have attempted in the main to follow a 16-year-old child-rearing adolescent whose dominant concern was to find her biological father. As a psychoanalytic clinician, I endeavored to understand her intrapsychic conflicts about skin color and how her core concerns fitted into her developmental vicissitudes. She used a Euro-American distortion about skin color as a determinant of self-image and wove this misreading of skin color into a distortion of her own, thereby creating a personal and idiosyncratic myth with a personal but overdetermined meaning. We have here Ms. T.'s unresolved agenda with her own father evolving in Fay's intrapsychic concerns. Fay's own concern about skin color eventually evolved in her cathexis of her son as a "cross" (hybrid) between light skin color and her father's dark skin color (a symbolic compromise!). The therapeutic strategy for helping Fay negotiate change in her functioning and in her world view was in the emphasis placed on the uncle–father's fathering over and above his being father as biological fact. In this respect I follow the thesis that family and psyche mediate reality and that the goal of the psychoanalyst or the psychoanalytic observer is to mediate psychic reality and to provide an opportunity for a person or family to renegotiate intrapsychic myths and other fantastic distortions.

Heinz Hartmann (1958) aptly writes:

> Man does not come to terms with his environment anew in every generation; his relation to the environment is guaranteed by— besides the factors of heredity—an evolution peculiar to man, namely, the influence of tradition and the survival of the works of man. We take over from others (prototypes, tradition) a great many of our methods for solving problems. . . . The works of man objectify the methods he has discovered for solving problems and thereby become factors of continuity, so that man lives,

so to speak, in past generations as well as his own. Thus arises a network of identifications and ideal-formations which is of great significance for the forms and ways of adaptation. [p. 30]

Hence, we can conceive of psychoanalytic discovery as, among other things, a mediation between deferred action and theorizing about history in fantastic or mythical ways by our patients. This process constitutes a psychic restructuring that permits us to enable our patients to overturn those stable and confining self descriptions that stunt their development as persons. After psychoanalytic interventions that challenge patients not to simply delineate their world but to overturn confining structures of experience, they can now freshly experience rather than simply repeat.

In this clinical illustration the four sets of juxtapositions in the system of mutual implications can thus be shown. In terms of the child's smallness and her adult sexual interests, Fay demonstrated this by shunning baby dolls in favor of the more fully grown and sexual Barbie dolls. In terms of the adult's physical maturity and his accompanying emotional immaturity, Uncle Abe, the incest perpetrator, stated that he saved the victim's life when she was young and on the brink of death and as such her body was his to own or transgress. When we look at how fact and theory appear and disappear together, we see in Fay's idiosyncratic myth that light-skinned blacks are sneaky a masking and a transvaluation of an anterior event with all the embroideries of contemporary ideas about skin color. As to trauma as remembered, the immanent aspects of the trauma get condensed, symbolized, and displaced in a way that shows us that Fay's mother was the first victim and now Fay herself has become a second victim although she was not *phy*sically transgressed. Fay was *psy*chically transgressed, and to protect herself she needed to revise her shared transgression with the stable but confining idiosyncratic thought that she must not trust light-skinned blacks. Treatment sought to and succeeded in overturning this myth. Further details of treatment are reported elsewhere (Stein and Apprey 1987).

REFERENCES

Barzun, J. (1985). The critic, the public, the past. *Salmagundi*, Fall, 1985–1986, pp. 68–69.

Ferenczi, S. (1933). Confusion of tongues between the adult and the child. In *Final Contributions to the Problems and Methods of Psychoanalysis*, pp. 156–167. London: Hogarth Press, 1955.

Foucault, M. (1972). *Archaeology of Knowledge*. New York: Harper and Row.

Freud, S. (1900). *Interpretation of dreams. Standard Edition* 4/5. London: Hogarth Press and the Institute of Psycho-Analysis.

Green, A. (1973). Le double et l'absent. *Critique* 312.

Hartmann, H. (1958). *Ego Psychology and the Problem of Adaptation*. New York: International Universities Press.

Khan, M. M. R. (1983). *Hidden Selves*. New York: International Universities Press.

Kris, E. (1956). The personal myth: a problem in psychoanalytic technique. *Journal of the American Psychoanalytic Association* 4:653–681.

Laplanche, J. (1987–1989). *New Foundations for Psychoanalysis*. Trans. D. Macey. Cambridge, England: Basil Blackwell Ltd.

Mahler, M., Pine, F., and Bergman, A. (1975). *The Psychological Birth of the Human Infant*. New York: Basic Books.

Mead, M. (1950). *Male and Female*. London: Victor Gollancz Ltd.

Merleau-Ponty, M. (1964). Maurice Merleau-Ponty à la Sorbonne. Resumé de ses cours établi par ses étudiants et approuvé par lui-même. *Bulletin de Psychologie* 17:3–6.

Pruyser, P. (1983). *The Play of the Imagination*. New York: International Universities Press.

Ricoeur, P. (1974). *The Conflict of Interpretations. Essays in Hermeneutics*. Evanston, IL: Northwestern University Press.

Stein, H. F. (1981). Personal communication.

Stein, H. F., and Apprey, M. (1987). *From Metaphor to Meaning*. Charlottesville, VA: University Press of Virginia.

Volkan, V. (1984). *What Do You Get When You Cross a Dandelion with a Rose?* New York: Jason Aronson.

White, H. (1989). Figuring the nature of the times deceased: literary theory and historical writing. In *Future Literary Theory*, ed. R. Cohen, New York: Routledge.

Winnicott, D. W. (1951). Transitional objects and transitional phenomena. In *Collected Papers: Through Paediatrics to Psycho-Analysis*, pp. 229–242. London: Tavistock.

7

VICTIMS OF INCEST

Discussion of Apprey's chapter, "Psychical Transformations by a Child of Incest"

M. Hossein Etezady, M.D.

Reading Dr. Apprey's chapter was a pleasure, especially since it provided me with the opportunity to share my reflections in considering a few of the many areas of potential elaboration that this multifaceted chapter opens. Dr. Apprey's material combines and integrates fascinating strands from psychoanalytic theory, technical consideration, and clinical application. Reading it, I found myself eager to anticipate each sequence, and as in reading a good suspense story, I found myself treated to a surprise ending, a treat not commonly associated with scientific works. One reason for my surprise, perhaps, had to do with the particular aspect of incest and its pathogenesis addressed in this paper. Victims of incest encountered in treatment are often individuals who had their unfortunate experience either early in their childhood or during the preadolescent or adolescent period. In the course of treatment, the incestuous involvement is either eventually reported or analytically reconstructed and uncovered. Children, however, who are themselves *products* of incest, such as Fay, are not as frequently reported or as readily thought of as "victims" of incest. They are nevertheless most certainly victims, conceived under one of the most aberrant of pathological and family circumstances. The imprint that such tragic beginnings leave on the psyche and on the core identity of these individuals will influence and alter the entire course of their psychological development. Born with this indelible vulnerability, these infants are then doomed to further victimization by the consequences of family and parental pathology. They experience more than their own share of deprivation, rejection, abandonment, foster placement, physical and sexual abuse, and other such misfortunes. The expectable vicissitudes of ordinary life and other traumatic experiences that we all expect to confront are only the top of this enormous burden. We can only hope that the favorable constitutional endowment and lifesaving resiliency that some children are gifted with may combine with the relative benevolence of environmental circumstances, plus access to help and timely intervention, so that some of these victims may have a chance at psychological survival.

When I casually polled my colleagues, no one could readily think of patients they had treated who, like Fay, were *products* of incest. In contrast, treatment accounts of children, adolescents, and adults who at one time or another had been the unwilling or victimized objects of incestuous sexual activity were practically countless.

Fay was not a direct object of incestuous exploitation. The fact that she was a product of incest gradually came to light as Ms. T. was eventually able to come to grips with her shame and guilt, aided by empathic support and gentle persuasion from Dr. Apprey. The suspense and drama that preceded and accompanied this emotionally charged revelation by Ms. T. was matched only by Fay's reaction of disbelief, dismay, and rage and her sense of betrayal.

We may wonder, along with Dr. Apprey, what will happen to the old defenses and fantasies that once sustained Fay. What new defenses might now be erected. What is the fate of her separation anxiety and mistrust in others? What will the quality of her relationship with her mother, the uncle/father, her son, and her boyfriend be? Although the answers to these important questions are relegated by Dr. Apprey to another time, it may be reasonable to *speculate* that the course of the transference, its development, working through, and resolution, will determine the direction in which these issues will evolve. The transference itself, needless to say, would depend on the quality of early object relations.

In Fay's case we have a complicated picture. Fay and her three siblings were born to an unmarried young mother. They were then placed in the care of Ms. T.'s older sister, whose husband sired these children. These factors alone would combine to pose a serious challenge to the fate of object relations. We have no information on whether this woman knew her husband had fathered these children, how she felt about this, and how this knowledge may have affected her attitude toward the children. It appears, however, that this woman did not challenge Ms. T. as the primary object of maternal identification for her children.

On the question of the effect of multiple maternal figures on the course of object-relations in children, Selma Kramer has shown that when the role of the mother is not challenged by conflicting competition from the substitute mother, the positive aspects of the experience with the substitute caregiver coalesce around the primary identification with the mother and will complement it. For Fay, it appears this was the case and as such, can be considered a favorable factor. Additionally, since Ms. T. lost her own mother at the age of 8 and was subsequently rejected by her father, her capacity for mothering and empathic attunement would be in serious doubt. The availability of another woman to do the actual mothering can therefore be regarded as another favorable factor.

From the observation by Dr. Apprey that Fay quickly dismissed the question of breast feeding with the answer, "It isn't me," we learn about her self-concept. That she felt like an "imposter." That she feared she would pass on to her child, through breast feeding, dangerous components of food she had consumed. She feared the baby would, in greed, scoop out the content of her breast. This sadomasochistic scenario featuring the archaic dyad of the baby's devouring greed and the mother's poisonous breast bespeaks of unneutralized aggression and unresolved ambivalence toward her mother, predisposing Fay to depression and threatening her relationship with her child. From this quality of object relationship, we may assume ambivalence and hostile dependence in all significant attachments, including that which would evolve and crystalize within the treatment and in the transference. The transference manifestation of these preoedipal issues brings to life conflicts, arrests or fixations, and the affective components that were the building blocks of early internalizations and structures.

It is also in the transference that powerful but subtle nuances of the separation–individuation process will be observable. These include but are not limited to the aggressive and libidinal cathexis of the self and the object, the wish to fuse with the idealized mother of symbiosis, the dread of being engulfed by the devouring and sadistic maternal introject externalized in the person of the analyst, the wish to magically control the dyadic partner, the wish to share in the illusory omnipotence of the idealized object, the rage of disillusionment and the despair resulting from having to relinquish the idealized object, the transmuting internalization of the consistent and positive features of the real relationship, leading to the diminution of symbiotic longings, the rage and the mournful process of loss of omnipotence, and, most important, the gradual and repeated juxtaposition of fantasy versus reality, internal versus external, love versus hate, and loss versus gain—characteristic of the rapprochement subphase. Optimally this should lead to neutralization of primitive aggression. Affects are thereby rendered controllable. Self and object representations are consequently more stable. Separation, autonomy, and competition are tolerable. Triadic relations, empathy, mature morality, and sublimation become achievable.

Margaret Mahler's (1984) familiar subphases of separation–individuation are normally negotiated within the matrix of maternal libidinal availability, predictability, and constancy. Similarly, in the therapeutic situation, empathic attunement, emotional availability, and constancy are essential for therapeutic alliance and the expression and working through of the forbidden aggressive and libidinal impulses. Positive treatment outcome depends mainly on the effective management of the transference. The foundation of this success, however, has been laid long before the treatment begins—during early childhood, based on the quality of the early experiences with the first libidinal object. The closer to optimal this relation was, the more optimistic the treatment prognosis will be.

The first object relationship (with the mother) is perpetually relived and reworked, influencing all subsequent relations. This, of course, equally applies to the relationship with the father. It is not surprising that Fay's view of her fantasied father is that he is not to be trusted and that he is "sneaky." Fay hates him for sneaking out on her and abandoning her, and she also hates her mother for protecting him by hiding his identity. In fact, from Fay's point of view, unworthy of trust and sneaky would more aptly describe the characteristics of the mother, since it was the mother who was the source of the concealment. She was the one who participated in creating and maintaining the mystery and the myth that Fay's father was light-skinned. Fay's image of her fantasied father was cast in the mold of her perception of the mother.

Fay's derogatory view of light-skinned blacks, supported by cultural reinforcement, reminds me of my experience with many black patients, children and adults, in the inner city where family disruption, poverty, and shattered images of self predominated. I repeatedly encountered the conviction in these individ-

uals that their color, light or dark, was what made them bad. If
an individual was scapegoated in a family, this self-view displaced on the color of the skin was obligingly reinforced by
other family members. In a young black adolescent boy whom I
treated from age 10 to 14, this phenomenon was striking. At age
10, he was depressed, beset by self-doubt and self-loathing,
feeling unloved, angry, and persecuted. At the end of his treatment, he was, in contrast, buoyant, self-assured, inquisitive, and
popular. Laughing at his own old theory that no one loved him
because he was "dark and ugly," he could now admit that his
mother and stepfather did love him, were proud of his recent
accomplishments and that he felt good about himself. He con-
ceded that his female cousins were right in describing him as
"cool and kind of cute." I wonder, then, whether Fay's derogatory attitude toward light-skinned blacks didn't express self-
deprecation, negative self-image, and narcissistic vulnerability.
Perhaps she used this cultural myth to split off her bad self,
projected in her view of the fantasied father.

　　Turning to Ms. T. as a victim of incest, we find all the
familiar hallmarks—a vulnerable and emotionally deprived
child, feeling rejected by her own father after the death of her
mother at age 8. She wanted to become pregnant in order to feel
loved and wanted. She was then exploited by her sister's husband. Ms. T's sister and her husband provided a ready-made
oedipal triangle, the sister representing the lost mother and the
husband representing the rejecting father. As incestuous relationships go, this was not a true parent–child or even sibling
incest. There was no blood relationship, and therefore the usual
inhibitions guarding against incest were relatively weak. The
role of collusion by Ms. T.'s sister, who raised three of these
children, cannot be underestimated.

　　The tragedy of incest is in the devastation that it causes the
victim. The shame and guilt of participation, the trauma of
being betrayed, violated, and used, and the loss of the sense of
integrity, feeling soiled and damaged forever, profoundly affect

the victims' emotional and social lives. This "ultimate betrayal" by an adult loved and trusted by a helpless and dependent child is what Shengold (1989) has called "soul murder." The scars are permanent and deep, and the consequences transgress barriers of generations. Children who are sexually abused, often at the hands of family members, have parents who have been sexually abused. Victims relive their trauma repeatedly through sexual acting out, self-victimization, prostitution, perversion, and the victimizing of children. They have major deficits in the development of their drives, ego, superego, and object relationships. Their capacity to establish intimacy, regulate their self-esteem, and modulate their affects are severely impaired. They suffer from a multitude of psychological and somatic disorders.

Most victims do not receive adequate help, and many are severely traumatized when the tragedy comes to light. They are subjected to examinations, evaluations, interrogations, separation from family and siblings, and disruption in their support system. When victims are able to get adequate help, the results can be highly rewarding. Dr. Apprey has already made mention of the tools that we need in order to understand and deal with the psychical transformations that result from the need to fill the gap created by the incestuous invasion. The resulting discontinuity is repaired through illusions, myths, and mystification, which treatment aims to resolve. The following excerpts from a seven-year analysis of a 25-year-old woman are used to illustrate these points.

A CASE OF INCEST

During the early part of the analysis, I was impressed with the intensity of the patient's anger, fear of rejection, guilt, and the need to be perfect. She needed to be friendly, charming, obliging, and admired by everyone. She was very sensitive to indications of criticism and could never criticize anyone. Her anger was often indirectly expressed in phobic or obsessive symptoms. During excitement and emotional arousal, she would experience choking, breathing problems, and fear of swallowing her tongue. She couldn't say "no" to anyone. She had a carefully concealed view of herself as being better than everyone else, the strongest, smartest, most beautiful, and most desired. What she felt as her own impulses, she disavowed and could not admit. Her dreams meant nothing to her and her "associations" were meaningless to her. These dreams presented themes of competition, jealousy, anger about feeling left out, and derivatives from her relationship with her father, mother, and sister. Fantasies of physical entanglement were also present in these dreams. Once I had helped her see how she couldn't acknowledge her wishes, and felt ashamed, guilty and afraid that no one would accept her because of them, and that she was concerned about what I might think if I knew about her, she brought into the analysis her first "erotic dream," which caused her great discomfort. She dreamed that I was approaching her on the couch, reaching out to hold her seductively, and urging her to forget about being analyzed. She could acknowledge superficially that this was a wish, that she liked me, and from all that was unsaid, she could see no faults or shortcomings in me. In fact, she was on her best behavior herself. She didn't want me to know her as the manipulative, hostile, teasing, controlling "dizzy blonde" she had been to everyone else. She wouldn't tease and act seductively, and would display nothing that I could find fault with. She began to become more and more rigid, anxious, stilted, void of affective expression, and unable to do any more than go through the motions. She had great difficulty in sharing with me the day-to-day involvements in her life, as if she feared that I would disapprove. I pointed out to her that her tremendous concern about my disapproval indicated that she herself didn't feel right about her own wishes and feelings, and it was she and not I or her mother who disapproved. This provided the opportunity to elaborate on her relationship with her parents. She had been the father's favorite. She often sat on his lap while he fed her honey. She felt amorous toward the father, wanted all his attention all the time, and was repeating the same experience and expectations in her relationship with me. She wished to sit on my lap and be fed sweet words and affection, yet she felt tense, guilty, and too ashamed to really face up to her longings.

My comments were met with complete compliance and further dutiful elaboration. However, I had an uneasy feeling of not being able to reach her. I felt she was carefully controlling me by telling me nothing in spite of giving the appearance of working hard. She was not talking with me, but cleverly misleading and confusing me. I felt she was continually neutralizing and frustrating me, as she felt "about to be pinned down or caught off guard." Rape fantasies, being forced into fellatio and fighting, hurting or being injured were recurrent themes at this time. As I commented on this, she felt insulted and accused of being a tease, which she had tried to conceal completely and hide from my view in the analysis. Evidence of rage then began to surface in her dreams of stabbing, killing, exploding or burning my house, and putting me in different emergency rooms after car accidents, which frightened as well as embarrassed her. The occasions for these gigantic waves of anger were numerous, as when she felt frustrated with me for not treating her as special, or as she felt jealous of my family and other patients, or during separations, holidays, weekends, and vacations. The only external expression of these waves of rage (which flooded her ego) was that she turned cold, her resort to withholding and experiencing no reaction, as if nothing I said or did reached her. At the same time, she was frightened that I would catch her off guard with her emotions bare. At all cost, she needed to hide everything she could. Hiding her hostility and her need to defeat, destroy, and render me helpless became a matter of life and death. She feared she could kill me or leave me or that I would reject, abandon, or harm her for her hostility toward me. Her fear of being abandoned forced her into attempts to control me by raising my curiosity, stirring up concern in me, and provoking me into attempting to rescue her. As with her mother, if she "innocently" led me to chase her suspiciously and anxiously or (as with boyfriends and her own father) charmed and seduced me with my heart in my hand, she could feel safe and less frightened of being abandoned. In her battle of wills in the mother transference, she needed to outsmart and outmaneuver me. Her most potent weapon against the mother had been the possession of a secret that she could safely protect. Letting her mother know or have any knowledge of what was on her mind was dangerous. In this context, for example, she couldn't tell me what she thought, planned, intended, or desired. In fact, everything in the first four years of the analysis was wrapped around this central theme of keeping the mother from knowing through the most effective means she could muster, namely "not knowing" herself. This defense in itself was elaborately camouflaged with layers of pseudocompliance, passivity, and anxious watchfulness. If she were stupid and the victim, she would be blameless and her mother would not leave her. Also passively, she could sit on her father's lap, being fed honey, yielding to as much as the father cared to do, and have no responsibility for what occurred.

The sexual teasing that was patterned after her relationship with her father demonstrated her wish to seduce her father into becoming excited and then to rape or force fellatio on her. Interpretation of this clarified various aspects of her defenses and made her aware of her sexual impulses and urges. She would then try to move on into the acknowledgment of her sexual feelings. This, however, would result in regression to the negative mother transference, and conflicts of control, autonomy, secretiveness, battles of will, fear of abandonment, and defensive clinging. With each episode of forward movement and appearance of derivatives of sexual urges in the father transference, there would be a marked regression characterized by freezing, detachment, and withholding. Once again, massive denial and pseudoimbecility would take over.

In the fourth year of the analysis, when the mother transference was extensively analyzed and the separation anxiety fueled by her hatred toward her mother was worked through, she was then in a position to deal with the father transference. The anxiety that this produced was overwhelming. This dramatic explosion of symptoms and heightened level of anxiety seemed to be a close replica of the patient's childhood neurosis. During that time, with her numerous symptoms and severe anxiety as a child, she had been hospitalized. The hospitalization was severely traumatic. Parting from the parents each day, the patient would dissolve into a profound state of panic. She would scream, plead, and weep all night. She had to be forcibly peeled off from her parents, as she would cling to them for dear life and didn't want to be left behind. This had been a long-standing symptom, causing her panic when she was outside of her parents' sight. It also extended into her school years as school phobia and well into her adolescence. One important determinant of this anxiety was her expectation at this time that with the development of complicated emotional reactions within her, she would have to enter frightening areas into which she had never allowed herself before. At that time, both of us being in the dark about her forbidden sexual fantasies and the attendant anxieties, could only register with bewilderment her paralyzing expectation of being abandoned and her defensive, desperate clinging. We had also learned by now that her sexual fantasies were so conflicted and such a source of guilt and shame that she could not allow herself any acknowledgment of them. The intensity of the excitement and the ensuing guilt was too overwhelming and flooded the patient with helplessness and panic. In retrospect, I now realize that I was not empathically in tune with the patient at this point. Not understanding or even completely "believing" the degree of her disorganizing distress, I kept on urging her to do better and more, attempted to make up for the "stalemate" through my own increased activity. The more I tried, the less she took notice, thereby provoking further activity and desperate intrusive measures on my part in order to reach her. I increased the pressure on the patient in my comments and interpretive interventions to the effect that she wanted me to chase, trap, invade, and overwhelm her as if in a fantasy of being raped. She kept provoking me, through her passivity, forcing me to do more and more as she remained cold, distant, unaffected, and unaware of my activity. If she were oblivious to my frantic activity, she would not have to feel guilty. This closely tied in with her sexual frigidity, which, in the same manner, caused her to be cold, uninvolved, and unaffected. She would tease and excite her sexually inhibited boyfriend (a closet homosexual) into intercourse. I showed her the ways in which she reacted to the analysis as she did to sexual intercourse. She secretly received gratification from this sexualized process, but could not allow herself to *know* about it. As the outcome of this difficult phase of the analytic work, the patient finally dared to become curious. She proceeded to request her records from the hospital where she had been hospitalized at age 6. What was contained in these records provided us with the missing piece that allowed for the possibility of the reconstruction of the infantile neurosis and understanding of her symptoms. This finally led to the resolution of the transference neurosis, with concomitant symptomatic relief, which ushered in the terminal phase. The startling information that developed from these hospital records was that the patient was traumatized twice in her first year: once when she was left to the care of her maternal grandmother at age 3 to 4 months, and then again at 12 months of age when her parents returned. The child had difficulty with both these transitions. She reacted with anger, obstinacy, and constipation and needed repeated enemas. She couldn't be left alone, was always antagonistic, and continued to have a very poor relationship with her mother. She was precocious and seemingly mature in many of her ways. Overactivity was a serious problem. According to these records, on her return the mother had decided to sleep with the patient's sister, as her husband had slept with my patient until before the hospitalization at age 6.

The wish to sleep with the father and be an inseparable and beloved possession to the idealized and maternalized father in a relationship devoid of any disappointment or hurt, as well as any sexual implication as acted in with the transference, could now be understood for the first time. Being asleep, nonresponsive, not responsible, and unaware of what went on was indispensable for the continuation of the fantasy. Awaking and being aware of the reality was not possible or tolerable due to the attendant excitement and guilt. In the transference, she could not "wake up," as this was equated with the termination of the abandonment of the relationship, of having nothing, being finished, as well as the acknowledgement of her incestuous wishes with all the guilt that permeated every aspect of the patient's personality.

This development provided us with more than factual information about the history. It furnished me especially with the orienting direction that led to my empathic and clear understanding of the patient's unusual responses of detachment, passivity, and pseudoimbecility. I could now understand the special meaning of my patient's freezing, being easily flooded, "not knowing," lack of differentiated affects, amnesia, her profound separation anxiety, and other symptoms. I realized that due to traumatization and the overstimulation caused by sleeping with her father, and perhaps the possibility of incestuous involvement with him, I was dealing with a damaged and overwhelmed ego that didn't possess the channels of discharge and defensive operations that can develop only through adequate neutralization of the primitive instinctual drives, mediated by parental empathy. The rest of the analysis went relatively smoothly, albeit slowly. From several dreams with breasts, tubes, milk, germs, biting, and excitement, a constellation emerged that indicated that the patient's disgust of milk was related to her wish–fantasy of fellatio, as if nursing on the penis. Talking to me and experiencing pleasure in the analysis was equated with performing fellatio on me. Expression of any anger meant castrating me with her oral sadism. Her "I don't know" defense was a defense against such oral aggression. As she developed the ability to express rage, jealousy, frustration, and her wish to destroy me, her love and tender feelings toward me could also be expressed. As she began finally to free-associate, she repeatedly found herself cold and distant. She was unable to talk, "not knowing" why, and found that she was so angry that she could not let herself know. This anger was too severe and "too crazy." She began to victimize her boyfriend in an unconscious displacement of her transference rage. I emphasized the wish behind her fear of biting my penis when she was angered in her unconscious fantasy of nursing on my penis in place of her own father's. This caused further

stirring, anxiety, and considerable depression. The patient often
sarcastically commented on my having caused her depression.
She had never before felt depressed, the myriad of her previous
symptoms notwithstanding.

At this time, the boyfriend decided to end his frustrating and
stalemated relationship with the patient. She was shocked and
enraged. This occurred at a time when she least expected it.
Analysis showed that she had unconsciously set herself up to be
rejected at a time when I had been struggling to show her that she
was doing all she could to provoke me into becoming frustrated
and dismiss her from treatment in anger. In retrospect we learned
that before terminating her analysis, she needed to practice getting
rejected and going through a trial mourning process in preparation
for the inevitable loss of the idealized father in the transference.

This convincingly showed the patient that she intended to
force me actively into abandoning her, much as she had been
abandoned during her childhood. She could now clearly see her
need to turn the tables on me and to do to me what she had
passively suffered in her childhood and what she expected I
would do to her if she were not the aggressor. I showed her how
her defense of identification with the aggressor threatened the
outcome of the analysis in that she was unconsciously aiming at
defeating the analysis by not becoming involved. Every session
from now on in some way revolved around her hidden wish to be
the one who would do the leaving and the hurting, rather than
being left or hurt. This was represented first and foremost
through her cold detachment and her continued use of the "I
don't know" defense.

This work led to the patient's ability to allow in her
consciousness the wish to masturbate her father and control him
into wanting and needing her while she was too frightened to
become sexually aroused herself. She could fantasize in vivid
detail about nursing on my penis. She could see herself as a little
girl between my legs as I played with her head, milk–semen
running from her mouth and on her face. Later, she was able to
experience this intense fantasy with her father in my place with

an eerie sense of vividness that convinced her that this was more than a fantasy or something that she had imagined. She was now certain that this and other fantasies of incestuous involvement with her father were memories that she had neither wanted nor could afford to recall. This was followed by material and dreams in which an enormous amount of hostility was directed at the father. Many memories and fragments coalesced to form a new and real image of her father in place of the idealized image of him she had always maintained. This was a very emotional period, strong affects now beginning to emerge clearly and intensely. The rage at the father who had taken advantage of her vulnerability and helplessness to seduce and sexually abuse her was beyond what she could tolerate. Her own guilt and shame and sense of worthlessness for wanting and pleasurably provoking her father was nearly impossible for her to confront. That her mother had put her in his bed due to her own frigidity additionally made her outraged at having been the innocent victim of disappointing and unreliable adults whom she had trusted and depended on.

It took a long period of time and much work to integrate and master all this material. The actual memories the patient recalled with frozen vividness and an eerie sense of reality were few. She struggled for the rest of the analysis to remember more. But she felt she just couldn't; it was too painful. She thought she still needed her father, who was by now old and sick and likely to soon die. She wanted, finally, to forgive her father. She felt he had done the best he himself could do under the circumstances of his life, and after all, he had only committed the one mistake, which couldn't be repaired at any rate. Perhaps she could tell her sister after her parents had died. But could her sister take such a shocking revelation about her father?

The terminal phase was highly productive. The remarkable success of the analysis was truly rewarding. For me, it was a profound and enlightening experience. And I hope it has helped elucidate some of the theoretical formulation.

REFERENCES

Byerly, L. J. (1990). Neurosis and object relations in children and adolescents. In *The Neurotic Child and Adolescent*, ed. M. H. Etezady, pp. 159–195. Northvale, NJ: Jason Aronson.

Dewald, P. A. (1989). Effects on adults of incest in childhood: a case report. *Journal of the American Psychoanalytic Association* 37:997–1014.

Etezady, M. H. (1987). Abstracts on the vulnerable child workshop: sexual abuse in vulnerable and high risk children. In *Child Abuse and Neglect*, vol. 2, pp. 461–474.

Furman, E. (1956). An ego disturbance in a young child. *Psychoanalytic Study of the Child* 11:312–335. New York: International Universities Press.

Glenn, J. (1990). Traumatic neurosis in children. In *The Neurotic Child and Adolescent*, ed. M. H. Etezady, pp. 59–74. Northvale, NJ: Jason Aronson.

Herman, J. L., Russell, D., and Tracki, K. (1986). Long-term effects of incestuous abuse in childhood. *American Journal of Psychiatry* 143:1293–1296.

Kaufman, I. (1982). Father–daughter incest. In *Father and Child*, ed. S. H. Cath, A. R. Gurwitt, and J. M. Ross, pp. 491–507. Boston: Little, Brown.

Kramer, S. (1986). Identification and its vicissitudes as observed in children: a developmental approach. *International Journal of Psycho-Analysis* 67:161–171.

Mahler, M. (1984). Symbiosis and individuation: the psychological birth of the human infant. In *The Selected Papers of Margaret S. Mahler*, vol. 2, pp. 149–168. New York: Jason Aronson.

Shengold, L. (1989). *Soul Murder*. New Haven, CT: Yale University Press.

Sherkow, S. P. (1990). Evaluation and diagnosis of sexual abuse of little girls. *Journal of the American Psychoanalytic Association* 38:347–369.

Steele, B. (1970). Parental abuse of infants and small children. In *Parenthood: Its Psychology and Psychopathology*, ed. E. J. Anthony and T. Benedeck, pp. 449–477. Boston: Little, Brown.

8

THE TECHNICAL HANDLING OF INCEST-RELATED MATERIAL

Selma Kramer, M.D.

This book gives testimony to analysts' increasing awareness of what might happen to the child if incest occurs. The authors demonstrate by clinical cases the emergence of incest material in treatment, as well as defenses against this emergence. They reveal their understanding of the conflicts that incest engenders. They offer an explication of psychoanalytic methods of treating incest perpetrators or victims. Steele (1990) provides us with reasons for the profound psychological residues in rape victims. He states:

The more dominance and violence the perpetrator expresses, . . . the more obvious is this exploitation [that is, the act is for the satisfaction of the perpetrator, not the child victim] and disregard. Yet, even in rape, the devastating consequences seem due more to the violence of the perpetrator and the relative helplessness of the victim than simply to the sexual aspects of the attack itself. Even in "milder" cases of sexual abuse, that is, where elements of violence, force, or cruel disregard for the feelings of the child are less prominent, the degree of trauma is related to the discrepancy between the intensity of the noxious stimulae and the ability of the child's ego to cope. The sexual experiences do not occur as isolated events in a neutral, standard background, but in a total context of the child's psychological development and the variable, complex family interactions. [p. 22]

Steele emphasizes that when the sexual exploiter of the child is the child's own parent, the effect of sexual abuse is much more devastating. The parent is relinquishing his or her role in providing comfort, help, and safety to this child, instead using the child for his or her own gratification.

Fischer's careful discussion of Steele's important contribution emphasizes that incest creates obstacles to normal development and points out the vulnerability of the child in the rapprochement subphase of the separation–individuation process. Fischer points out the complex developmental processes that occur in the rapprochement subphase; these account for the greater vulnerability of the rapprochement subphase child to inadequate parenting or to intrusive overstimulation by either parent. Significantly, she also includes in her discussion the need for fathers to be available emotionally to their mates and children. And among many important comments, Fischer emphasizes the rage of children who, helpless, are used by their parents for their own sexual gratification.

Of course, analysts wish to explicate the therapeutic processes that help undo the profound intrapsychic and interpersonal results of incest. However, there is no uniform analytic approach for incest victims. Their psychopathology varies greatly, from psychoneuroses, borderline and narcissistic phenomena, and multiple personality disorder to psychoses. Treatment must therefore be tailored to the patient's ability to trust, develop a therapeutic alliance, permit free association, explore memories and fantasies of incest, and eventually recall or reconstruct, hence master, the experiences of incest.

Should every person involved in incest be psychoanalyzed? No, this is neither possible nor feasible. However, we are concerned with the fate of those who receive no treatment at all, or who receive superficial treatment, such as short-term therapy, behavior modification (usually reserved for fathers who have come to the attention of the judicial system because of their incestuous involvement with their children), or group therapy (for incest victims). The tenacity of defenses against recognition and disclosure of the incestuous experience, the problems of self-esteem, basic trust, and the compulsion to repeat, as well as the complex transference–countertransference issues makes it appear that traditional psychoanalysis or psychoanalytic psychotherapy offers the preferred treatment. Clearly, this is only true as long as incest itself and associated noxious environmental factors (physical abuse, emotional neglect, alcoholism, abandonment, etc.) have not caused the incest victim to have psychopathology too severe for traditional analysis. However, even where analysis is not feasible, the theoretical and practical knowledge derived from psychoanalysis is invaluable in helping these patients. As we see in Chapter 7, John, a frightened, resentful adolescent who had participated in incest with his mother, started treatment under duress—a treatment that had little promise of becoming an analysis. However, Margolis's understanding of John's intrapsychic conflicts, and of the family dynamics that lead to incest, along with his empathic and sensitive handling of John's resistances and his proclivity to regress and act out (under stress and during interruptions of treatment), enabled him to guide, maintain, and strengthen a therapeutic alliance to the present time, when a "real analysis" is approximated. Steele's case reports reveal the neediness and immaturity of both parties involved in father–child incest and the pathology in families in which children are involved in parental sex. He observes, as does Margolis, that the actual acts of incest are often preceded by more subtle forms of sexual seduction, including bathing with parents, exposure to parental nudity, and parents' inappropriately sharing beds with children.

Margolis's second case is interesting in that his patient started analysis as a relatively successful woman, already in her fifties. This underscores the long-term characterological residues of childhood incest. Her need to know was sublimated to a great degree in successful accomplishments at school. However, it took the analysis to really let her know the most troublesome secret, the parental incest. Analysis also freed her from the need for repeated masochistic experiences, and at the same time helped resolve the psychopathological elements that contributed to her low self-esteem.

Akhtar's scholarly discussion of Margolis's chapter raises issues of whether the analysis should clarify the real-life events John experienced, in contrast to his carrying the cloak of "miracle child" and of his relationships to each parent. Akhtar also discusses diagnostic issues, including the potential relationship between incest and perversion. He compares the two cases presented by Margolis. Akhtar's profound questions should, I hope, result in further dialogue between the two analysts and stimulate additional psychoanalytic articles by each of them on this subject.

Apprey's chapter reveals the extremes of doubting and questioning in one of three children who were all products of a long-term incestuous relationship between their mother and their uncle. We might wonder why *this* child had such doubts and why her family romance fantasies took their particular forms, and what the source was of her fantasies about restitution by her father. Could she have carried in her unconscious her own mother's feelings of deprivation as a child when her (the mother's) father lavished gifts on his stepchildren and gave his biological daughter nothing? There is no answer to why this one of three siblings demanded that her doubts be relieved and know of her paternity. Was she more sensitive or brighter than her siblings?

Etezady's discussion of Apprey's chapter is especially informative. He describes with great candor the slow, painstaking process of an analysis in which one of his own patients used formidable resistances against the emergence of material concerning incestuous experiences with her father. Etezady also discloses his own countertransference problems in handling his patient's sadomasochistic fantasies. Transference–countertransference problems may be, I feel, especially difficult to deal with in analyses of incest cases.

While Steele, Margolis, and Apprey offer striking clinical material here, there still remains an overall lack of psychoanalytic data about incest. Why is it that relatively few psychoanalysts have written about incest? Freud's changing attitudes about incest in the pathogenesis of the neuroses no longer appear to be a valid reason for this state of affairs. I am inclined to believe that because of analysts' own blind spots concerning incest, because of countertransference issues to their patients' transference, and because instructors who supervised training of today's analysts did not recognize or even suspect incest, many incest cases go unrecognized. I have noted that antipathy to recognizing and working with derivatives of incest to be especially great in cases of maternal incest (children who had been masturbated by their mothers from infancy, often until adolescence). Such countertransference-based reluctance can often lead either to a superficial treatment or to the patient's dropping out of the treatment altogether. If patients leave treatment in which incest is unrecognized and with continuing personality problems and unresolved intrapsychic conflicts, they often seek treatment with another therapist to relieve their continuing intrapsychic pain or to help them minimize their tendencies to act out. Of seven "incest" patients in treatment with me in recent years, four had been in prior treatment, with a total of seven prior therapists.

Continued experience in the conduct of psychoanalysis, greater comfort with the disclosure and working through of disquieting historical and conflictual elements in our patients' analytic material, and increased reliance on our countertransference will make us better able to treat these cases. Despite such reminders, our own resistances in recognizing incest-related material persist. This was evident in the fact that when I presented material about maternal incest at psychoanalytic meetings, my audiences often seemed perturbed and ill at ease. They accepted maternal incest only if it had occurred in families of low social and economic status. They were shocked and unbelieving when I described socially stable and economically well-off Caucasian families in which the fathers were middle-class professionals and the mothers had at least a high school education. In general, they seemed to attribute more serious pathology to mothers who molest their children of either sex than to fathers who sexually molest their daughters. I feel that further studies on incest may explain whether this is actually so. Are we inclined to let fathers "off the hook," as if to say "boys will be boys"? I suggest that the well-known sentiment that mothers should be pure and virginal, far removed from sexual interests in general and from sexual desires for their children in particular, could be the reason for this. Possibly, the average mother is more inhibited than is the father in acting out sexual fantasies with their children.

I hope that this book will lead us to consider further questions. Are there patterns in the analyses of certain patients that might make us suspect that incest has occurred although the patient has not made any overt mention of it? Are there common pitfalls to which analysts should be alerted in analyses where incest has occurred? How should incest material be handled?

Most of my patients, regardless of the sex of the abusing parent, evidenced depression, low self-esteem, conflicts over their dependency needs (usually greater than in other analysands), somatic symptoms of hyper- or hyposensitivity, problems with basic trust, learning problems, and a tendency to doubt their own perceptions as well as the veracity of the analyst. An extreme of this doubting appears in children used sexually by their mothers from infancy on, taking the form of what I refer to as "object-coercive doubting." This form of doubting is predicated on the lack of self-object differentiation at the time of the incestuous experiences. It makes the child coerce the incestuous parent or her substitutes (the analyst in the transference and often the teacher at school) to argue one of the opposing sides of the child's intrapsychic conflict about knowing. Incest victims very often feel guilty, and carry the blame and shame for the act. This is often because the parent who perpetrates the incest denies responsibility, at times blaming the child or even denying the act (Ferenczi 1933). Our patients also report, or show in the transference, episodes of unexpected anger. Most of my patients have had separation problems and poor peer relationships. Over the years I have felt that these separation problems occur in maternal incest because of inadequate mother–child differentiation, which itself stems from the mother's need to maintain her child as a symbiotic partner. In paternal incest, separation problems and poor peer relationships may be the result of the child's low self-esteem, of his or her extreme needs to be dependent on one or the other parent. A parent may actively take a stand against the child's befriending other children, possibly out of a fear of losing access to the child or because of the danger of the child disclosing the incest.

Disclosure of incest by the child who has been sexually seduced usually takes place fairly late in analysis, unless the patient has been referred by the court, as in Margolis's case of John. Amnesia of the incestuous experiences, persistence of pathological defenses such as "vertical splitting" (Shengold

1974, 1989), which permits conscious awareness to coexist with defenses against acknowledgment (to the self or to others) that incest had occurred, the threat of personality disintegration, the fragility of the ego, and the proclivity to act out or to regress all militate against the emergence of recollections of incest until the analysis has considerably strengthened the ego. In addition, there must have been ample attenuation in the analysis of super-ego distortions, the pathological identifications with the parents having been replaced by healthy identifications with the analyst and with other healthy objects in the environment. Therefore, much needs to be accomplished in the transference before the ego and superego permit the patient to admit having been a partner in incest, even in dreams and fantasies.

Williams (1987) emphasized the need for reconstruction by the analyst of early incest, saying "In . . . a seduction at an early age which led to a severe neurosis, no conscious recollections can be obtained" (p. 146). She referred to Freud (1918), who said that "[scenes that] further lay claim to such extraordinary significance for the history of the case, are as a rule not reproduced as recollections, but have to be divined . . . reconstructed gradually and laboriously from an aggregate of indications" (p. 51). I feel that reconstruction must evolve from many sources. These include the constellation of the associative material, the structure of the analysis that leads the analyst to recognize pathological defenses against free association, the nature of transference material, the patient's dreams and fantasies—all evolving from the patient's conflicts over the emergence of this material and from conflicted self and object representations. Verification by the analyst that incest has occurred affords great relief, for "at last someone understands and believes me," as one of my patients said. As Shengold (1989) says, "Trying to define what can be known and remembered about these seemingly historical events, trying to get the patient to differentiate memory from fantasy, is part of what must be done in therapy to undo the brain-washing inherent to soul murder" (p. 40). Shengold feels that the therapist must attempt to answer the question, "Did it really happen?" I have found the questions, "Did I want it to happen?" and "Did I enjoy it?" to be often even more troublesome to the patient. Answers to these questions are frequently much more disturbing than the verification that the incestuous act happened.

I wish to address two additional issues that have been suggested by the preceding chapters in this book. The first pertains to the relative culpability of each parent (regardless of which parent had incestuous experiences with the child), and second, to whether incest can ever be an advantage to the child. My experience is that incest occurs only in a markedly dysfunctional family. Maternal incest, as I have reported it in young children, takes place in a family where pathology is rampant. The mother is possessive, but only intermittently gratifying; as she was overinvolved with her own mother, so is she overinvolved with her child. The father, usually very passive, with a poor sense of self, is emotionally distant from both his wife and his child. Alcoholism and poverty were *not* significant familial factors in my "maternal incest" cases. In paternal incest, while the father is held responsible for the act, the mother is considered equally responsible and very culpable by some authors (Bigras 1990, Browning and Boatman 1977, Finkelhor 1979, Steele 1990). In cases where the mother had conscious knowledge of the incest or where she encouraged her daughter to continue an incestuous relationship with the father in order to placate him or to extract money or gifts from him, the mother is both disturbed and responsible. However, where a mother is physically and emotionally ill and the father and child turn to each other, can it really be considered the mother's fault? Ruth Fischer in her discussion joins me in asking whether we hold mothers responsible for everything evil that happens.

Do analysts use sexist attitudes in suggesting that the mother is fully culpable in maternal incest and that she is also largely culpable where the perpetrator of incest is the father? If a mother is emotionally unavailable to the father, why is his alternative choice of his daughter as a sexual object so easily justified? Certainly, in the best of all worlds, both parents are mature, reliable people who are available to each other as partners and lovers and are available to their children as parents, fulfilling their parental function of loving them, but nonsexually, and of providing them with physical and emotional support and protection. We react with discomfort when either parent fails to honor the incest barrier, but we find the mother at fault in each instance! Clearly, more thinking is needed here.

Additional attitudes I should like to question are those of Margolis (Chapter 4) and Shengold (1989) that their patients benefited from incest. To suggest that incest is better than nothing suggests that "nothing" represents chaos, abuse, and deprivation in a family with rampant psychopathology. I am reminded of a patient in treatment from prelatency well into adolescence for a symbiotic psychosis from which he gradually emerged. When an adolescent, he disclosed how much he had envied his sister, who was beaten by his mother while he had been ignored. He said poignantly, "At least she got some attention!" He went on to ruminate whether being fed poison (being beaten) was better than being starved. I suggest that we are in a dilemma similar to that of my patient when we speculate whether incest is preferable to indifference.

In the same vein is Margolis's contention that his patient, John, by virtue of incest with his mother, was better off than his brother. The fact is that with the exception of financial status, John's brother seems to be better off in every way. He is described as being less conflicted and not given to John's outbursts against others or to self-destructive episodes. Can it be that John's being "better off" is a second family myth? (The first myth involved portraying John as the miracle baby who lived, although he was not expected to survive his premature birth.) Are we as analysts sharing in parent–child denials or distortions? John survived physically; that his emotional life was compromised from the beginning was suggested to me when I heard that as an infant John was remote and not cuddly. (Salman Akhtar also makes this point in his discussion of Margolis's case.) I suspect that it was easier for John's mother to be an adequate nurturer of his much more responsive brother when he was an infant.

CONCLUSION

I wish to conclude with thanks to the three main contributors (Apprey, Margolis, and Steele) and the three discussants (Akhtar, Etezady, and Fischer) for their important contributions. They have shared with us a rich portrayal of the multigenerational aspects of incest and suggest that without intervention, incest often repeats itself with the former victim as the perpetrator. Recent contributions to developmental literature by Sroufe (1980, 1986) attest to this. He alludes to studies that revealed that "spousification" had occurred, that is, that parents who themselves had been exploited by a parent abused their own sons and daughters. While the *manner* of the abuse of their children was not identical to what their parents had done to them, the *meanings* were the same. In some cases, fathers' abuse of their daughters may cause these daughters (even after treatment) to continue to interact with their fathers in an erotic, secretive fashion even though overt sexual activity has stopped between them.

There are so many who must be made aware that incest is inimical to normal, healthy development. Actually, psychoanalysts are not the first line of defense here. The first line consists of parents, who may need help in being honest about what they are doing with their children and to face the truth of their mate's behavior vis-à-vis their children. The next line of defense to protect children from incest is comprised of family physicians, pediatricians, school nurses, or others who as health professionals are in regular contact with the child. In our positions as experts in the field of emotional development who are called upon to diagnose and treat severe psychopathological processes, it behooves psychoanalysts to function in these very important areas of prevention and early intervention. By addressing psychopathology of incest, we are making an important inroad into the prevention and amelioration of the profound psychological trauma—the trauma of transgression—caused by the use of a child's body for the sexual gratification of the parent.

Note: I thank William Singletary, M.D., for the references to Sroufe.

REFERENCES

Bigras, J. (1990). Psychoanalysis as incestuous repetition. In *Adult Analysis and Childhood Sexual Abuse*, ed. H. Levine, pp. 173–196. Hillsdale, NJ: Analytic Press.

Browning, D., and Boatman, B. (1977). Incest: children at risk. *American Journal of Psychiatry* 134:69–72.

Ferenczi, S. (1933). Confusion of tongues between the adult and the child. In *Final Contributions to the Problems and Methods of Psychoanalysis*, pp. 156–167. London: Hogarth Press, 1955.

Finkelhor, D. (1979). *Sexually Victimized Children*. New York: The Free Press.

Freud, S. (1918). From the history of an infantile neurosis. *Standard Edition* 17:48–60.

Shengold, L. (1974). The metaphor of the mirror. *Journal of the American Psychoanalytic Association* 22:97–115.

——— (1989). *Soul Murder*. New Haven, CT: Yale University Press.

Sroufe, L. A., and Fleeson, J. (1986). Attachment and the construction of relationships. In *Relationships and Development*, ed. W. Hartup and Z. Rubin, pp. 51–71. Hillsdale, NJ: Lawrence Erlbaum.

Sroufe, L. A., and Ward, M. (1980). Seductive behavior of mothers of toddlers. *Child Development* 517:1222–1229.

Steele, B. (1990). Some sequelae of the sexual maltreatment of children. In *Adult Analysis and Childhood Sexual Abuse*, ed. H. Levine, pp. 21–34. Hillsdale, NJ: Analytic Press.

Williams, M. (1987). After-effects of early seduction. *Journal of the American Psychoanalytic Association* 35:145–165.

Index